WATERSIDE
In Yorks

The Yorkshire Dales,
West and South Yorkshire

Len Markham

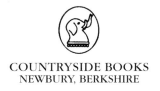

COUNTRYSIDE BOOKS
NEWBURY, BERKSHIRE

COUNTRYSIDE BOOKS
3 Catherine Road
Newbury, Berkshire

To view our complete range of books,
please visit us at
www.countrysidebooks.co.uk

ISBN 1 85306 605 2

Designed by Graham Whiteman
Cover illustration by Colin Doggett
Photographs and maps by the author

Produced through MRM Associates Ltd., Reading
Printed by J. W. Arrowsmith Ltd., Bristol

Contents

AREA MAP SHOWING THE LOCATION OF THE WALKS

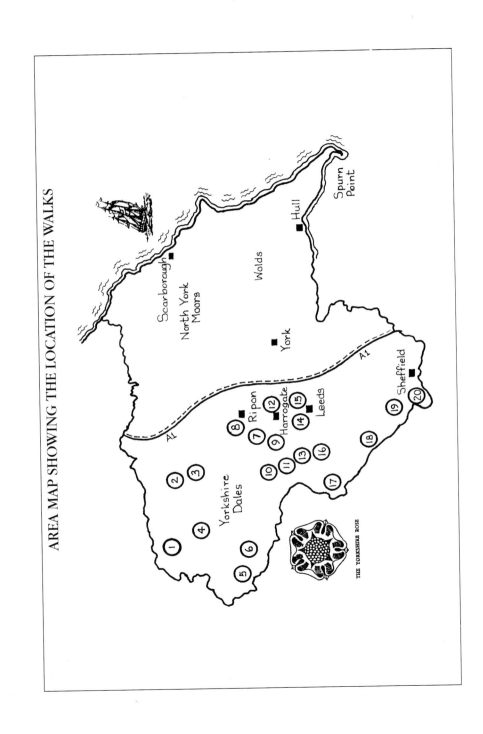

THE YORKSHIRE ROSE

Walk

❦

PUBLISHER'S NOTE

We hope that you obtain considerable enjoyment from this book; great care has been taken in its preparation. Although at the time of publication all routes followed public rights of way or permitted paths, diversion orders can be made and permissions withdrawn.

We cannot of course be held responsible for such diversion orders and any inaccuracies in the text which result from these or any other changes to the routes nor any damage which might result from walkers trespassing on private property. We are anxious though that all details covering the walks are kept up to date and would therefore welcome information from readers which would be relevant to future editions.

INTRODUCTION

Water in Yorkshire has long meant more than the means of a monthly bath. The indigenous populations in these parts revere anything that fills pockets 'wi' brass' and our famous chalybeate water was a liquid commodity that in days gone by had more cachet than champagne. Not that we natives drank it, you understand. God forbid, it tasted foul! No, we saved it for the poor invalids from London who came north in their droves for the Yorkshire cure . . . bless 'em.

The world famous spa in Harrogate had 87 wells, their efficacious waters promising cures for everything from scrofula to malaria. Hydropathic institutions also grew up in Ripon, Boston Spa, Ilkley and Ben Rhydding. No wonder that the Yorkshireman has an affinity with water.

I will give you a taste of this liquid gold in our tour of Yorkshire waters. We will visit both Harrogate and Ilkley, extending our itinerary to find waterside routes along some of the finest rivers in the north: the Swale, Ure, Nidd, Wharfe, Skell, Aire and Rivelin – rivers that have nurtured majestic abbeys, guarded impregnable castles and turned the wheels of industries that made England great. Bounded by the Great North Road – the A1 – in the east, our walking canvas encompasses the Dales, and West and South Yorkshire, featuring not only rivers but diminutive and little known lakes, ponds, becks, streams, cloughs, fosses, forces, falls and reservoirs. These vintage waters are served up with stunning scenery and an aquatic history that includes two cataclysmic floods, grisly drownings at one of the most dangerous beauty spots in England and the conquering of the country's deepest shaft. We will follow in the footsteps of kings, monks, drovers, lead miners, philanthropists, industrialists and TV stars and I am sure that you will like me, have a host of adventures along the way.

As far as practicalities are concerned, none of the walks are too taxing, varying between 2 and 8 miles in length. All are within the capacity of both young and old and the only requirements are stout, preferably waterproof footwear and warm clothing.

For the added convenience of walkers, most walks start from or near a pub or pass one en route. Details of some wayside cafés and teashops are also given, although it should be stressed that all such information is subject to change. Telephone numbers are provided so that you can make advance enquiries about menus and opening times. It is often possible for customers of a pub to leave their cars in the car park while they walk, but the landlord's permission should always be sought first. If you want to park by the roadside, please make sure that you consider local residents and be careful not to obstruct any exits or entrances.

Brief details of places of interest within a short driving distance of each walk are included too, to help you plan a full day out if you wish.

Using the simple to understand route descriptions allied to the sketch maps, all the walks are easy to follow, although for further enjoyment the quoted Ordnance Survey Outdoor Leisure Series or Landranger maps are recommended. These are particularly useful for identifying the main features or views.

In walking these routes, may I ask you to follow the Countryside Code, always keeping to the proper paths, closing all gates, keeping dogs on leads and being particularly vigilant about litter. Remember, the best walkers leave only footprints!

Finally, I dedicate this book to good old Yorkshire rain without which this book would not have been possible.

Len Markham

KELD: SWALEDALE WATERFALLS

This route in the outer limits of Swaledale offers you giddy drops and stupendous views, cataracts, waterfalls, splintered rocks and the ghostly ruins of abandoned mines and workings – a walking experience indeed!

The Swale Valley

At over 1,100 feet above sea level, the tiny, remote hamlet of Keld is an ancient farming and mining settlement set in a dramatic landscape, the very names of its ravines and hills giving a squareness to the jaw and a glint to the eye.

Beginning in Keld's square, the walk crosses the river Swale above the waterfall of Kisdon Force, following the valley side to the wonderfully named Crackpot Hall and Buzzard Scar. The narrowing path then thrusts deep into the side valley of Swinner Gill, crossing a waterfall before plunging due south, then using a more sedate track along the river bank to the crossing point at Ramps Holme Bridge. The return route accompanies the river back to Keld.

The old books refer to Keld's Cathole Inn but the towels must have been draped even before I was born and my party remained thirsty. However, a short way back down the valley on the B6270 is the village of Muker and the unspoilt Farmers Arms. With wooden seating, flagged floors and open fireplaces this welcoming pub serves lunchtime and evening snacks, the typical fare including beef and gammon steaks, lasagne and fried cod. The house beers are Theakston, John Smith's and Nimmo's bitters. Opening times Monday to Saturday are 11 am to 3 pm and 7 pm to 11 pm. Sunday hours are 12 noon to 3 pm and 7 pm to 10.30 pm. Telephone: 01748 86297.

- **HOW TO GET THERE:** Keld is in an isolated position at the head of Swaledale. Ideally the walk should be part of a planned overnight visit to the area to justify the mileage involved and the long journey times from the larger towns and cities. The main access is from the east along the scenic B6270 from Richmond.
- **PARKING:** There is only limited parking in the small square at Keld. At busy times, park outside the village and walk in.
- **LENGTH OF THE WALK:** 6½ miles (anyone suffering from vertigo should avoid this one). Map: OS Landranger 98 Wensleydale and

Waterfall above Kisdon

9

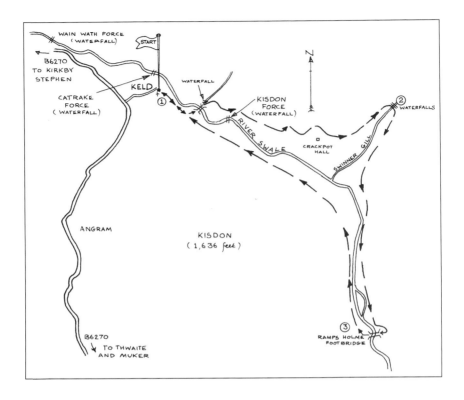

Upper Wharfedale and 92 Barnard Castle or OS Outdoor Leisure 30 Yorkshire Dales Northern and Central areas (Keld GR 893012; Muker inn GR 910978).

THE WALK

1. Turn right from the square in Keld, following the signposted track to Muker, and after a few hundred yards go left, following the Pennine Way sign over a ravine on a footbridge. Walking to the left of the waterfall, climb up the slope and swing right over the bridge at the top of the falls, swinging right through a gate and continuing at the top of the gorge on a track arcing left. Keep on the well-defined track passing ruins and abandoned workings and gradually swing left at the foot of the hill on a narrowing path into the side valley of Swinner Gill. Keep going until you have reached a point high above the falls and drop down to the falls.

2. Carefully cross the Swinner Gill, regain the path and swing sharp right out of the valley passing further waterfalls on your right. Drop down towards the Swale, going left on a bankside path. Walk on for just under 1½ miles and then fork right to the footbridge and cross right.

3. Follow the well-defined track left for about 2½ miles through a series of stiles and gates back to Keld.

PLACES OF INTEREST NEARBY

The natural wonders of this area eclipse everything that's man-made. North-west of Keld are the further waterfalls of *Catrake Force* and *Wain Wath Force* and there is an abundance of further exciting walking to *Clumpstone Hill, Great Shunner Fell, Rogan's Seat* and other eminences to delight a whole convention of boot makers.

MARSKE: MAY THE FORCE BE WITH YOU!

Alexander Livingstone would have loved the Marske Beck. A miniature Nile it isn't but there is something about following its banks through a wooded gorge that will bring out the explorer in you. All hush and gurgle, this short and leisurely walk to the splendid waterfall of Orgate Force has a Brigadoon magic, such is the isolation of this unspoilt off-shoot of Swaledale.

The Marske Beck

An enchanting village with an ancient church and a delightfully kept old hall with fine water gardens, Marske has no refreshment stop but the Bridge Inn in nearby Grinton on the main Swaledale road will provide for all your needs. On the old pack horse route beside the Grinton Beck and opposite the Cathedral of the Dale – St Andrew's 12th century church – the Bridge offers open fireplaces, hearty bar and restaurant meals and accommodation. Typical walkers' refreshments include variously filled baguettes, fresh fish, home-made soups and scrumptious home-made sausages, honey roast ham and roast chicken. The house ales are John Smith's and Black Sheep and Theakston from the Masham Brewery. Opening times are Monday to Sunday 12 noon to 11 pm (10.30 pm on Sundays). Telephone: 01748 884224.

- **HOW TO GET THERE:** Marske is in Swaledale, north-west of Richmond. Take the A6108 west from Richmond for about 4½ miles, turning right just before the B6270 fork.
- **PARKING:** Park at the bottom of the hill on the parking area near the bridge.
- **LENGTH OF THE WALK:** 2½ miles. Map: OS Landranger 99 Northallerton and Ripon and OS Outdoor Leisure 30 Yorkshire Dales Northern and Central areas (walk parking area GR 104004; inn GR 046984).

THE WALK

1. Go left from the parking area and cross the Marske Beck on the bridge.

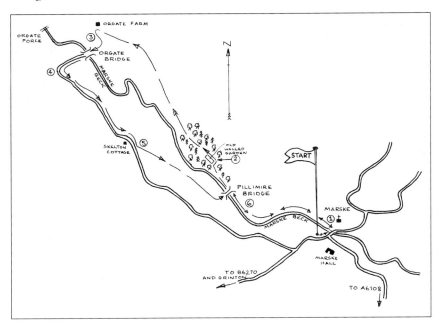

It's easy to ignore such a utilitarian but elegant structure. Probably dating from the 15th century, it has chamfered ribs.

Turn left through a gap in the wall, descend the steps and follow the path beckside up a further flight of steps and through a gate, continuing to Pillimire Bridge.

In connecting two fields, such a large and substantial structure looks out of place until you take a peep over the parapet and discover a massive abandoned water wheel.

Walk on to the gate and go through into the wood, following the well-defined path. Swing right uphill to the gate and go through.

2. Go left on the track by the old wall and at the path fork keep going straight forward, leaving the wood and going through a gate.

Notice the towering cliffs to the right.

Go through a further gate and proceed towards Orgate Farm.

3. Go left opposite the farm on a descending concrete track back towards the beck and cross the footbridge over the Marske Beck.

From the footbridge you can see the merry Orgate Force. It is in private ownership and public access is not encouraged.

Continue uphill on the metalled lane.

4. Swing sharp left on the quiet lane and walk on for about 800 yards, going left 20 yards past Skelton Cottage, through a gap in the wall downhill towards the beck.

5. Cross a meadow diagonally right, heading for the prominent telegraph pole, to a stile. Go over and follow the fence down alongside and above the beck to the Pillimire Bridge and go left over the bridge.

6. Turn right on the lower track and retrace your way back to the start.

Orgate Force

PLACES OF INTEREST NEARBY

Marske Hall was once the home of the Hutton family. The Archbishop of Canterbury Dr Matthew Hutton was born here in 1692. The family is remembered in the delightfully situated church of *St Edmund's* on the hill. It has a Norman doorway and box pews. Nearby is the interesting and attractive market town of *Reeth*. Its *Swaledale Folk Museum*, charting the history of the local lead mining industry and other fascinating aspects of local life, is open from Easter to October. Telephone: 01748 884373.

MIDDLEHAM: ALONG THE URE

With its high gables and narrow cobbled yards ringing to the sound of hooves, Middleham still has the feel of a garrison town, its superb views tugging at your boot strings at every turn. Beginning in the bustling market square, our path takes us through St Mary's and St Alkelda's churchyard, dropping down to the banks of the incomparable Ure and on to Wensley, the village that gave the dale its name. Leaving the river, the track climbs to the high moor where, in sheer exuberance at the vista, you can join the racehorses on an afternoon gallop.

View across the Ure towards Bolton Hall

This romantic 'Windsor of the North' sits imperiously above the river Ure, its castle and associations with the young King Richard III still radiating a regal air. Sweep the horizon from the battlements with your telescope and you will enjoy a panoramic history of England; towers, stately halls, ruined abbeys, ancient churches, and a hallowed piece of ground where Mary Queen of Scots was captured after her escape from Bolton Castle, all crowding the lens.

A centre for tourism and horse training, Middleham has an inviting collection of craft and speciality shops, cafés, restaurants and inns. In the shadow of the castle, the Black Swan is one of the cosiest. With a split level oak-beamed bar and an intimate dining room, it serves a wide range of home-cooked meals, some braised in local ale. The typical menu includes beef in 'Old Peculier', Yorkshire gammon, chicken and ham pie and popular griddled steaks. The house ales are from the Theakston stable – Bitter, XB and Old Peculier. The inn is open on Monday to Friday from 11.45 am to 3 pm and 6.30 pm to 11 pm, on Saturday from 11 am to 11 pm and on Sunday from 12 noon to 3 pm and 7 pm to 10.30 pm. Telephone: 01969 622221.

- **HOW TO GET THERE:** Middleham is near Leyburn on the A6108 north-west of Ripon. The easiest access is from the A1 at Leeming Bar and then onto the A684 to Leyburn.
- **PARKING:** Park in the market square.
- **LENGTH OF THE WALK:** 8 miles. Map: OS Landranger 99 Northallerton and Ripon or OS Outdoor Leisure 30 Yorkshire Dales Northern and Central areas (inn GR 128878).

THE WALK

1. From the square, go north for a few yards on the Leyburn road and turn left, following a signpost to the church.

There is much here to detain you. According to legend, St Alkelda was a Christian Saxon princess murdered in AD 800. Pilgrims came to Middleham to visit her holy well whose waters were said to cure problems of the eye. See part of her tombstone, other fascinating memorials within the church and also the plaster impression of the Great Seal of Richard III.

Go straight forward through the churchyard and through a gap in the boundary wall, crossing a field and steering right. Go through a second wall gap across a second field and cross the turning area near the new housing, swinging left to a stile. Cross and go through a wicket gate, continuing straight ahead over a meadow. Keep right over the next field to a gate and go through 10 yards left, going left again through a gap in a wall. Follow the yellow arrow sign veering right, keeping in the bottom, to a gate. Go through and swing right, crossing the stepping stones over a small stream to a gate. Go through and follow

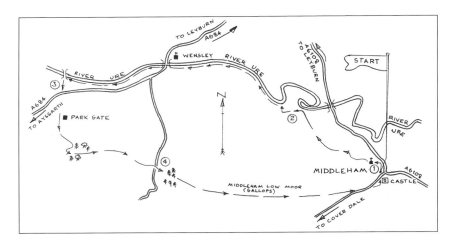

the wall down towards the river and go through a galvanised gate, swinging right and left to a gate. Go through and turn sharp left on a track.

2. Two hundred yards before the barn, turn sharp right towards the Ure, following the line of an old hedge for 100 yards. Go left over a culvert and then go through a gate, swinging broad left to the river bank. Continue to Wensley Bridge.

Near the bridge is Holy Trinity church. Packed with ancient treasures, it dates from the 13th century. Inscribed with a date of 1394, the brass of Sir Simon de Wenslaw is particularly fine. See also the 'carvings' of bored altar boys on the pews!

Go left up the embankment and cross the A684, dropping down to regain the riverside track. Continue and just before Lords Bridge, weave left to a gate. Go through this and a gap in a wall and go left on a track known as Bay Bolton Avenue.

3. Walk uphill, cross the A684 and keep straight ahead on the access to Park Gate Farm. Swing left and right uphill into woodland and at the top of the treeline keep to the left-hand side of the wall and go through a gate, heading to the right of a barn. Swing right to the topside of the wood and swing left through a gate, following the wall to a gate. Go through and continue at the lower side of Spigot Lodge Plantation to a gate and the road.

Middleham and its ruined castle

4. Go through the gate, cross the road, go through another gate and continue for 60 yards, turning right over a stile into Millers Gill Plantation. Veer right diagonally and leave the wood, crossing a stile. Keeping in the same general direction, look out for a gap in the wall. Go through and pick up the broad equestrian training track on the top of Middleham Moor. Continue on this to the outskirts of the town and go left to the road. Cross and steer left to the wicket gate. Go through and follow the public footpath sign and the wall left at the back of the castle. Go through another wall gap, cross a stile and veer left to a gate. Go through and swing left into the town and swing right in front of the castle and left back to the inn.

PLACES OF INTEREST NEARBY

Middleham Castle is open from April to September. Telephone: 01969 623899. As equally stirring is the still lived in *Bolton Castle* (west of Leyburn) with its reminders of Mary Queen of Scots. See the recreated herb garden. Telephone: 01969 623981. South-east of Middleham (nearly opposite *Jervaulx Abbey*) is *Brymor Ice Cream Parlour* – contented cows and forty flavours! Telephone: 01677 460377.

SEMERWATER: LAKESIDE PEACE AND CRAGGY HEIGHTS

Memories of this legendary and most romantic of all Yorkshire lakes have the pull of a spring tide. Come here once and be smitten forever. Ancient tales speak of a city of gold beneath the waves but the real treasure is to be found in the beauty and solitude that brought the Quakers to live on the shores of this natural glacial lake. Such is the compelling hush hereabouts and a palpable spirituality heightened by the lapping of the waves, the sighing reeds and the sight of a roofless chapel and rows of sad gravestones, that a simple walk here is imbued with a wash of meditation.

Semerwater

Fed by the Marsett and Crooks Becks, Semerwater lies at the entrance to lonely Raydale. In turn, the lake feeds the shortest river in England, the Bain that gives its name to the flourishing market town of Bainbridge. The scattered population of Raydale resides in the three tiny hamlets of Stalling Busk, Marsett and Countersett, the latter settlement keeping its Quaker chapel, an atmospheric and simple building that exquisitely captures the mood of this walk. The chapel is open to visitors. Our route skirts the lake and passes through all three hamlets, rising steeply to the heights overlooking the Roman road known as Cam High Street.

The absence of licensed premises in Raydale seems wholly appropriate and you will need to repair to Bainbridge for nourishment of a more bodily kind. Overlooking the village green, the inviting Rose and Crown flaunts its age, the inscription above the porch 'AD 1445' bidding us a warm welcome. The altered interior retains some old woodwork and a notable frieze and houses the famous Bainbridge Horn. This was traditionally blown in winter as a guide to travellers. The inn serves daily specials such as chicken curry and home-made steak and onion pie, its staple dishes including the ever popular gammon and eggs and fried cod and haddock. The house ales are John Smith's, Webster's and Theakston. Opening times Monday to Saturday are 11 am to 11 pm. Sunday hours are 12 noon to 10.30 pm. Telephone: 01969 650225.

- **HOW TO GET THERE:** Semerwater is some 3 miles south-west of Bainbridge off the A684 Leyburn to Hawes road. The easiest access is through Countersett.
- **PARKING:** Designated parking areas (fee payable) are available on the north side of the lake.
- **LENGTH OF THE WALK:** 6 miles. Map: OS Landranger 98 Wensleydale and Upper Wharfedale or OS Outdoor Leisure 30 Yorkshire Dales Northern and Central areas (Semerwater parking area GR 922876; inn GR 934903).

THE WALK

1. From the parking area, go south-east along the verge to a farm and, opposite the buildings, turn right over a stile, following a footpath sign to Stalling Busk. Keep to the low side of the meadow and go through the wicket gate, steering left to a gap in the wall. Go through to a second gap in the wall and continue through, passing a barn. Drop down to the fringes of the lake. On a well-defined path, go through a further wicket gate and a succession of wall gaps and a gate to the ruined chapel.

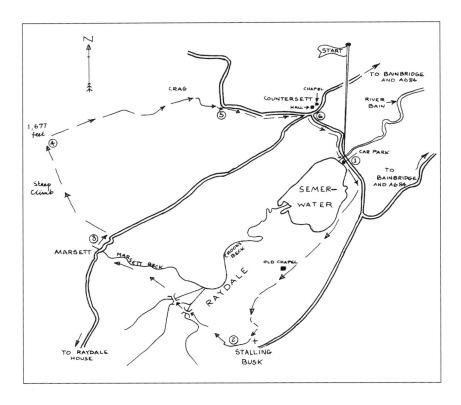

This sizeable chapel was originally built in 1603 and rebuilt in 1722. Among its ancient gravestones are several touching modern memorials.

Follow the Stalling Busk signpost uphill away from the lake, go through a gate and up a steep hill by a wall and go through a wicket gate into Stalling Busk, turning right past the tiny church of St Matthews.

The church was built in 1909 to replace the abandoned chapel. See an old chapel photograph inside.

2. Turn right down a track – Busk Lane – for about 200 yards and go right again through a gap in the wall, following a public footpath sign for a few yards only, then going left down the long meadow. At the intersection of tracks, keep going forward and left to find a footbridge over the beck. Cross and walk on to the next footbridge, arcing left by the Marsett Beck to Marsett village.

Just south of Marsett is Raydale House, the highly unlikely setting for what is regarded as the last act of domestic warfare in England. In a land dispute between the Metcalfes of Nappa Hall and the Robinsons of Whorton, the house was besieged from the 4th to the 7th June 1617 and one man was shot dead. The leader of the attackers, Sir Thomas Metcalfe, was arrested, fined £1,000 and imprisoned in the Tower of London.

3. Turn right over Marsett Bridge and go left after 200 yards, following an upward track signposted to Burtersett. After 300 yards, fork right over a stile and steer right to a gap in the wall. Go through, climbing steeply to the summit of the hill.

4. Go right along the top, heading towards the crag, and weave down right on the prominent path underneath the scar to the bottom. Swing right to a gate and go through to a second gate, arcing left to the road bend.

5. Turn right on the quiet road into the hamlet of Countersett.

The prominent Quaker Richard Robinson lived in Countersett Hall and George Fox, the founder of the Society of Friends, is known to have stayed there. The chapel is just below the hall.

6. Retrace your steps back to the junction and turn left on the steep road back to Semerwater and the parking place.

Places of Interest Nearby
In nearby Hawes is the *Dales Countryside Museum*. Its exhibits, ranging from flints to furniture, tell the fascinating story of the dales people and their landscape. Telephone: 01969 667450. Also in Hawes are the premises of *W.R. Outhwaite, rope makers*. There are daily displays of the rope maker's craft and a range of goods for sale. Telephone: 01969 667487.

CLAPHAM: POOH STICKS
FOR THE GODS

The Gods created the deepest shaft in Britain so they could out-do Pooh Bear. Join them in the game. Drop your sticks down Gaping Gill and rush the two miles to Ingleborough Cave to see who's won. But you may have to wait a while. The country's most famous pothole has over seven miles of passages!

Gaping Gill

Our classic walk begins in Clapham, only its name and connotations of loud applause and railway junctions ruffling the serenity of this very special Yorkshire outpost. We follow the Clapham Beck through a nature reserve estate developed by the 'Father of Alpine Rock Gardeners' Reginald Farrer, passing the visitor attraction of Ingleborough Cave, onward through the spectacular limestone gorge of Trow Gill to the mountain flanks of Ingleborough, one of Yorkshire's redoubtable 'Three Peaks'. The ultimate highlight of the walk is to peer into the black abyss and to drop your sticks, watching as the Fell Beck tumbles 365 feet. The return route uses an old drovers' track and two intriguing dark tunnels.

We set out from the splendid 18th century coaching house – the New Inn. Offering good accommodation and both bar and restaurant meals, this cosy hostelry has many memories of olden times, displaying photographs of potholers and hiking men, bills of past functions and sporting trophies. Its stalwart bar menu includes traditional Yorkshire puddings, Barnsley chop, steak in ale pie, Stilton and leek bake, ham and eggs, and fried fish, together with daily specials such as roast pheasant in season. The ale tally is Tetley and Dent Brewery bitters. Opening hours on Monday to Friday are 11 am to 3 pm and 7 pm to 11 pm. Saturday opening is from 11 am to 11 pm. On Sunday the inn is open from 12 noon to 3 pm and 7 pm to 10.30 pm. Telephone: 015242 51203.

- **HOW TO GET THERE:** Clapham is easily accessed, just ¼ mile off the A65 Skipton to Kendal road.
- **PARKING:** Park in the inn car park to the rear. If not patronising the inn, use the 'Pay and Display' facilities 200 yards up the road to the right.
- **LENGTH OF THE WALK:** 5½ miles. Map: OS Landranger 98 Wensleydale and Upper Wharfedale or OS Outdoor Leisure 2 Yorkshire Dales Southern and Western areas (inn GR 746692).

THE WALK

1. Go right from the inn and follow the lane alongside the Clapham Beck. Continue past the entrance to Ingleborough Hall, the former home of the Farrer family, to the church of St James the Apostle. Turn left over the bridge and go right, up to the head of the village, turning left at the 'Ingleborough Cave' sign and then right, following a similar sign, weaving right again past the cottage to the start of the nature trail, (small entry fee payable).

2. Follow the woodland path left and right to the lake.

This was created by the Farrers between 1828 and 1832, its seven acres and 48 million gallons of water providing power for a generator that brought street lighting to Clapham when much of London was in darkness! Did this inspire the distinguished scientist Michael Faraday, the son of the village blacksmith?

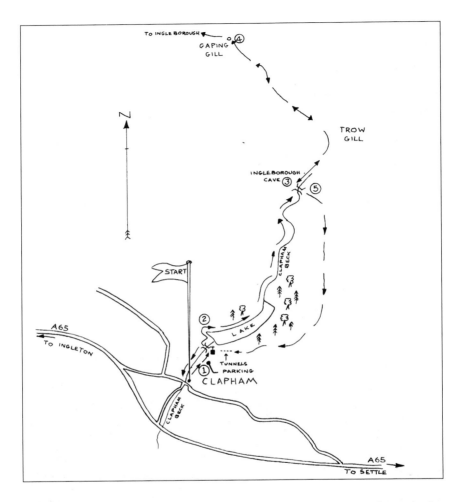

Pass the falls to the right and the belvedere to the left, go through the gate at the Ingleborough Cave sign and leave the wood, walking on to the cave building.

At this point the beck disappears into the hillside.

3. Continue forward on the stony track, cross a stile and veer left to Trow Gill, walking on through the gorge and up the rock scramble to the neck of the old falls.

The limestone gorge of Trow Gill

Glaciation is responsible for this splendid landscape. A little higher up, on the moor, see the distinctive limestone blocks known as clints. The spaces between are grykes.

Keep left by the wall and go left over the ladder stile on the moorland track towards Ingleborough. Swing right to Gaping Gill.

The pothole was first entered by Frenchman Edouard Alfred Martel in 1895.

4. Retrace your steps back to Ingleborough Cave and walk back towards the wood for about 300 yards, going left off the path just before the gate.

5. Go left over a footbridge and climb up wallside to a ladder stile. Cross and turn right on a track – Long Lane. Continue for about ¾ mile and go right at the track junction, following a track signposted 'BW Clapham ¼'. Go under two tunnels, weaving left past the churchyard and turn right past the church to recross the outward route bridge. Go left here and follow the beck down to the bridge, going left again over the bridge back to the inn.

PLACES OF INTEREST NEARBY
Discovered in 1837, the floodlit *Ingleborough Cave* has over ¾ mile of passages and caverns, its natural wonders including strange formations and stalagmites and stalagtites. Fee payable. Open daily from 1st March to 31st October. No vehicular access. Telephone: 015242 51242. Monuments and tributes to the Farrers can be found in the *village church of Saint James the Apostle*. Inside you can buy a fascinating booklet about Clapham's witch Dame Alice Ketyll. Near Clapham just off the A65 is the *Yorkshire Dales Falconry and Conservation Centre* housing a variety of raptors from around the world. Free flying displays, handling courses, lecture rooms, tea room and shop. Open every day from 10 am. Telephone: 01759 822832.

STAINFORTH: 'SMOKING WATERS'

Sensually stunning, the waterfall at Catrigg Foss remains untouched since the last Ice Age, its silver torrents, wreaths of spray and shafts of sunlight clashing like 'Star War' sabres, offering the visitor a mystical and elemental experience. Stand here alone and you will hear siren tongues, translated, the primeval name 'Smoking Waters' hanging on the breeze.

Above Catrigg Foss, looking towards Penyghent

This short walk from the village of Stainforth has Catrigg Foss as its destination, the route accompanying the Stainforth Beck part way before branching off to greet the moor and wonderful views of Pen-y-ghent and Fountains Fell. The return leg to the village is over a descending cart track.

The walk starts at the popular walkers' pub, the Craven Heifer, in the centre of the village overlooking the beck. With bed and breakfast accommodation and inviting rooms lit by colourful stained glass, the pub serves traditional fare such as steaks, Yorkshire puddings, steak and kidney pie, mixed grills and various roasts, and has developed a reputation over the years for old fashioned Yorkshire farmhouse teas. Bar top, there is a choice of Thwaites bitter and mild. Opening times Monday to Saturday are 11.30 am to 3 pm (closed Monday lunchtime in winter) and 6.30 pm (7 pm in winter) to 11 pm. Sunday hours are 12 noon to 3 pm and 7 pm to 10.30 pm. Telephone: 01729 822599.

- **HOW TO GET THERE:** The village of Stainforth is just over 2 miles north of Settle off the B6479 road signposted to Horton-in-Ribblesdale. Primary access is from the A65.
- **PARKING:** Park in the small car park opposite the pub or on local side streets.
- **LENGTH OF THE WALK:** 3 miles. Map: OS Landranger 98 Wensleydale and Upper Wharfedale or OS Outdoor Leisure 2 Yorkshire Dales Southern and Western areas (pub GR 822673).

THE WALK

1. Turn left from the inn and take the quiet lane signposted to Halton Gill, climbing up and turning right just beyond the Stainforth sign, following a footpath to 'Henside Road 1¾'. Walk along a track, go through a gate and veer left across a meadow with Stainforth Beck to your right, then swing left up a rise and drop down right to a concrete footbridge over the feeder stream of Tongue Gill.

2. Cross the footbridge, ignoring the path immediately to the left heading for the barn upstream, and walk on for 30 yards before turning sharp left through a wide gap in the wall, heading diagonally left away from the valley of the Stainforth Beck uphill over a long field. Head for the large rock in the middle of the field and keep in this general direction for about 800 yards, veering left towards a wall and a ladder stile. Climb and cross the second field, crossing the second ladder stile and heading slightly right towards the third field corner, going right at the corner following the wall down to the sheep fold. Mount the ladder stile and cross into the fourth field and go left then right in the middle of the field, dropping down and climbing up to the ladder stile in the left corner. Cross and keep to the top of the fifth field to a ladder stile and cross.

3. Turn right for 80 yards, following the wall down to a further ladder stile, cross this sharp right and aim left on the indeterminate path steering in the general direction of the wood on the skyline. Cross a

The 'smoking waters' of Catrigg Foss

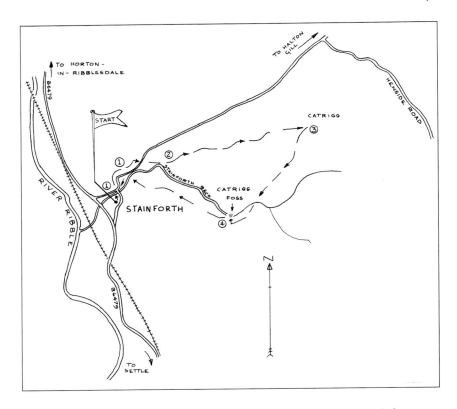

ladder stile and follow the wall down for 120 yards, going left over a ladder stile, keeping wallside and walking on to cross the Stainforth Beck feeder on a footbridge. Go right through the wall gap at the corner and walk on to the second wall gap, going through to a track.

At this point turn right and follow a distinctive path generally left a short distance to the cascades, signposted 'Catrigg Foss'.

4. Return to the main track, turn right and continue, dropping down back to Stainforth for just under ¾ mile. Go left into the village and turn right back to the Craven Heifer.

PLACES OF INTEREST NEARBY

Just south of Stainforth in a converted 19th century cotton mill alongside the river Ribble is the *Watershed Visitor Centre*. Fifty-two crafts are on display and there is a coffee shop. The centre is open every day from 10 am (11 am on Sundays). Telephone: 01759 825111.

GRANTLEY: THE QUEST FOR EAVESTONE LAKE

Such is the sinuous, often unmarked trail leading to one of Yorkshire's least known lakes that you may, like the classical Theseus, feel in need of a reel of thread to lead you from the labyrinth. But fear not! I will guide you to and from this grotto of the Gods.

Eavestone Lake

Eavestone Lake was once used by the monks of Fountains Abbey as a giant fish-pond. Its thickly wooded shores are hemmed in by weathered gritstone blocks whose contorted faces – snouts here, glaring eyes and fangs there – are from the same geological stock as those on the more celebrated monoliths at nearby Brimham Crags. But Eavestone's menagerie is far more sinister – contorted branches and leaves darkening the way and deep arboreal litter spiriting away the sound of every stride. Make sure **your** magic sword is well honed.

Crossing the narrow river Skell, the paths to and from the lake are through pleasant agricultural country with long distant views of the hills.

On a hilltop, Grantley (the name derives from a person who was dubbed 'the grumbling one') was once part of the huge estates of the de Mowbray barons who ruled the area from a long since demolished stronghold at Kirkby Malzeard. At the centre of the village is the inviting Grantley Arms, an almost traditional country inn that happily welds open fireplaces, low beams, real ale, home-made meals . . . and the internet! You can interrogate the daily specials menu from your computer choosing from such dishes as steak and kidney pie, spicy chicken breast and halibut in prawn sauce. The standard menu offers vegetarian alternatives and a number of beefsteak options including a New York speciality topped with bacon and egg. The house beers are Beamish Red and Theakston, Black Sheep and John Smith's bitters. Opening times Monday to Sunday are 12 noon to 3 pm and 7 pm to 11 pm (10.30 pm on Sundays). No food on Mondays or on Tuesday lunchtimes. Telephone: 01765 620227. Website: www.grantleyarms.co.uk

- **HOW TO GET THERE:** Grantley is west of Ripon and is easily reached on the B6265 Ripon to Pateley Bridge road. Turn off at Risplith.
- **PARKING:** Park in the inn car park or on the side lane where the walk commences.
- **LENGTH OF THE WALK:** 6 miles. Map: OS Landranger 99 Northallerton and Ripon (inn GR 233699).

THE WALK

1. Turn right from the inn along the cul-de-sac lane past the telephone box.

Note, on the right, the house adorned with a sculpted queen's head. This is the former village school endowed in 1712 by Johannis Richmond of nearby Skelding.

Continue to the end of the lane and go right by the farm entrance gate, following the public footpath sign through a gap in the wall. Swing right and go immediately sharp left through a gate. Follow a wall parallel with the farm buildings to a stile. Cross and follow the yellow arrow marker hedgeside to a second stile. Cross and continue forward to a third stile. Cross, keeping fenceside on a raised path and walk on to a corner and a fourth stile. Cross and follow the yellow arrow marker

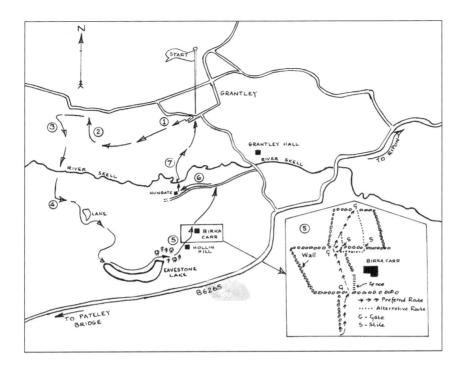

fenceside, passing in front of the renovated farmhouse and dropping down to a fifth stile and a small stream. Cross both, weaving right and swinging left hedgeside to the field corner. Turn left for 40 yards and go right on a farm track.

2. Steer right and go through the farm gate and the farmyard uphill, passing the farm buildings and swinging right on the access road. Continue climbing to the crest of the hill.

Go left through a gap in the wall, following the footpath marker, and cross the field, keeping straight ahead. Continue through a second wall gap and veer diagonally right over the next field to a corner gate. Go through left and head towards the farmhouse fenceside, proceeding through another gateway on a track, then going left over a stile into the children's play field in front of the farmhouse. Cross the field, heading for a yellow arrow marker on an electricity pole, and continue to a gap in the wall.

Go through and turn right on a track for about 100 yards. Go left – faint unofficial red arrow on the wall – through a wall gap into a

Giant gritstone blocks line Eavestone Lake

triangular copse. Keep fenceside for about 200 yards and leave the copse through a gap in the wall. Turn left on a concrete lane, following the tree-obscured bridleway sign, for about 300 yards. (From this point, for about the next 2½ miles until you reach Hollin Hill Farm beyond Eavestone Lake, the route is, untypically, very well signposted. Look out for yellow arrow markers in a distinctive six-pointed star.)

3. Go left along a track through a gate and continue to a second gate. Swing left downhill to a third gate, swinging right, then left, right and finally left downhill to the river Skell.

This is the fabled water that nourished Fountains Abbey. It rises a short distance to the west on Dallow Moor. The ancient crossing point in front has been replaced by a modern pedestrian bridge a little way upstream.

Go left through a gate and walk on for 100 yards. Turn right over the bridge and right again for a further 100 yards, crossing two stiles and turning left up the hill. Veer left, following the wall uphill to a stile. Cross and continue wallside.

4. At the point where the ground levels out, go left through a gateway wallside to another gate. Go through right fenceside on a depressed path, swinging right downhill towards an ornamental trout lake. Go left over a stream on a rising track through a gate and continue on through another gate. Swing left on a track and go through a gate, merging with a quiet lane and passing a cottage. Swing right, passing Grange Farm up a steep hill and drop down, going left.

Rise again and just before the steep climb, turn left on a woodland path, weaving right to the shores of Eavestone Lake.

Successive owners have landscaped the lake margins which are now thick with rhododendron. The lake supports a wide variety of wildfowl including coot, moorhen, grebe and tufted duck. The woods are home to siskins.

Continue following the path and at the end of the lake swing right by the shore on a causeway, crossing the humpbacked bridge and continuing straight ahead on a steep climb to the edge of the wood.

5. Cross a stile and steer diagonally left over a field (if in crop go round) to the corner. Go left and swing right through Hollin Hill farmyard to a gate. (The star arrow markers are absent from the rest of the route which is poorly signposted from this point.)

Go through the gate then swing left hedgeside and follow the wall round right towards Birka Carr farmhouse.

The next part of the walk is over the farmer's preferred route but he has also kindly indicated the alternative route (shown on the plan). Go left of the house through a first gate into a recreation field, following the yellow arrow marker to a second gate. Go through into a field, steering right and dropping all the while to a third gate at the mid-point of the wall.

Go through, then steer right over the field towards a telegraph pole, keeping right to a fence. Go left downwards to a stream. Cross this and a stile, continuing over the narrow neck of a field to a second stile. Cross and go left along a farm track.

6. Continue to the farm and the cottages at Hungate. The route turns right (left-hand side of the barn) for 10 yards towards the gated stockyard and then turns sharp right again through a gate for a further 10 yards to a yellow arrow marked support post on the right-hand side of the barn. Turn left here over a field to a gate and go through, dropping down slightly left over a field to find a white footbridge over the Skell.

7. Cross and go right over a stile alongside the river for about 100 yards on a slope then go left (marker on a post), heading for the corner of a wood. Cross a fence, heading diagonally right over a field to a hedge corner. Maintain your direction to the right-hand corner of the field and go through left. Keep fenceside heading up towards the village and veer left to a ladder stile. Cross and keep fenceside to a wicket gate. Go through and turn right along the lane back to the pub.

PLACES OF INTEREST NEARBY
Fountains Abbey, one of the most fascinating and historic religious sites in Europe This Cistercian abbey beside the river Skell and medieval deer-park has a visitor centre and offers guided tours. Telephone: 01765 608888. *Lightwater Valley Theme Park*, a 'heart in the mouth' extravaganza in 175 acres, is off the A6108 north-west of Ripon. Closed in winter. Telephone: 01765 635368. The least known attraction in the area is *Markenfield Hall* just south of Ripon. A fortified manor house described as one of the most romantic in England, it was built in 1310. Only open to the public on Mondays from April until October. Telephone Ripon Tourist Information Centre for details: 01765 604625, 01423 537300 in winter.

RIPON AND FOUNTAINS ABBEY: A PILGRIMAGE ALONG THE SKELL

Some architectural wonders are wont to trumpet their presence for miles, monumental gates, tree-lined drives and grand vistas beguiling the senses like honour guards and fanfares. For sensory experience, this wonderful route to Fountains Abbey can be compared to the finest palace entrances in the world, but it is far more sublime, leading from the shadows of Ripon's St Peter's Cathedral along the delightful banks of the river Skell and through Studley deer-park to the largest monastic ruins in Britain. The World Heritage Site of Fountains Abbey is indeed a great spiritual experience. Heighten that experience and come, like thousands of pilgrims before you, on foot.

The river Skell, with Ripon cathedral beyond

Ripon Cathedral has its origins in the 7th century when a monastery was founded in the town by St Wilfred whose Saxon crypt is believed to be the oldest in England. The cathedral has a host of other treasures, notably the misericords in the choir and a collection of cups, chalices, flagons and patens in the treasury. In addition to an array of interesting shops, Ripon has two unusual museums – the Prison and Police Museum and the Workhouse Museum. In the centre of the market square is a 90 foot high obelisk. Every night at precisely 9 o'clock, the City Hornblower sounds his horn at each corner of this monument, performing a ceremony that has been a nightly event for 1,000 years. The river Skell flows through the ancient precincts and passes within a toe's dip of the aptly named Water Rat.

A bright and airy modern pub with fine views of the river and the cathedral beyond, the Water Rat offers a range of standard fare including gammon and eggs, rump and sirloin steaks, cottage pie, pork and stuffing baguettes and salads supplemented by daily specials such as chicken in black bean sauce and fresh fish. This pub has a wide selection of beers – Mansfield Old Baily, Waggle Dance, Samson Smooth and Wards and Lambtons bitters. Opening times are 12 noon to 11 pm (10.30 on Sundays). Telephone: 01765 602251.

- **HOW TO GET THERE:** The Water Rat is south-east of the town centre, just off the B6265 (the road to the racecourse). Approach from Bondgate Green.
- **PARKING:** Park in the short side street outside the pub (dead-end, no vehicular access over the river) or nearby on the B6265 alongside Iddesleigh Terrace (near the City Motor Works).
- **LENGTH OF THE WALK:** 7 miles (plus any walk you may choose to do in Fountains Abbey grounds). Map: OS Landranger 99 Northallerton and Ripon (inn GR 315709).

THE WALK

1. Turn left from the inn on the riverside path, walking upstream under the Bondgate Green Bridge. Continue to the Bondgate Bridge and go left to Bondgate, crossing the road and going right and left to rejoin the riverside path. Continue along Barefoot Street.

At this point my young daughter spouts forth: 'All towns in the States are rubbish . . . all they have is 84th Street and the like . . . you wouldn't find a Barefoot Street in American now would you?'

Just before the A61 Harrogate Road junction, turn right through a gap in the wall and go left under the span, following the river upstream and

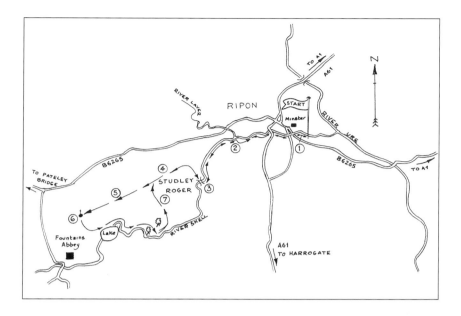

bearing left to the children's play area. Go through the play area and turn right on the lane. Follow the lane as it accompanies the river and continue to the confluence of the Skell and the river Laver.

2. Follow the Skell left and go up the waterside steps, continuing through woodland and gradually following the river south to a lane end. Turn right following a public bridleway sign over a stile to the Skell footbridge.

3. Cross and walk on a track to a gate and go left towards a house, crossing an ornamental bridge over a beck. Swing right fieldside, following a footpath sign to Studley.

4. Halfway down the field, turn left, following the sign across a field. Continue through a couple of gates into the village of Studley Roger.

5. Cross the lane and follow the public footpath sign through a kissing gate into the deer-park.

In 1818 it was described as being 'cloathed with large and beautiful timber, well stocked with deer and kept within lofty hedges and neat

The Water Rat pub seen here on the left of the river

borders shaven with the scythe and levelled with the roller.' Nearly 200 years on the natural wonders are undiminished. Here you will find heroic views, majestic oaks, sweet chestnuts and giant firs and a sight that will send all admirers of the longbow and the legendary Robin Hood into raptures. Browsing under great boughs whose ancestors gave England its victory at the Armada are hundreds of deer. Oblivious to the attentions of visitors, they wander freely, in the autumn and summer months engaging in the dramatic spectacle of the rut.

Continue along the green track going left to the road and go forward right along the tree-lined avenue past the estate office to the church.

A Victorian masterpiece commissioned by the Marchioness of Ripon, it commemorates the murder by Greek bandits of her brother, Frederick Vyner.

To visit Fountains Abbey, continue straight ahead through the gateway and swing left on the new footway signposted to the visitor centre.

This thoroughly modern centre offers a complete range of facilities including an imaginatively designed restaurant and a shop. Guided walks are arranged to the ruins and the water gardens which include temples, statues, ponds and cascades. Entrance fee payable.

After leaving the centre, retrace your steps back to the park.

6. Go through the gates and after 20 yards, turn right on the green track, forking right to a lake. Go left along the shore and swing right over a planked bridge. Weave left and right over a series of ornamental bridges down a valley and go through a kissing gate into a dense wood. Steer left on a track, gradually climbing. Leave the trees and emerge left on a farm track.

7. Continue forward into the village and pass the village hall. Turn right, following the footpath sign. Follow the outward route back to the pub.

PLACES OF INTEREST NEARBY

Ripon Cathedral is built on the site of St Wilfred's church of AD 672. Its Saxon crypt is believed to be the oldest such structure in England. Don't miss the 500 year old misericords and the cathedral treasury of cups, chalices, covers, flagons and patens.

DACRE BANKS: RIVER NIDD AND YORKE'S FOLLY

Passing old mills and converted farmhouses, our meandering walk down the exceptionally tranquil Nidd valley, after visiting a winery, assaults the bastion of Guise Cliff and Yorke's Folly. The return route skirts Heyshaw Moor before returning through quiet pastures to the village of Dacre Banks.

Nidderdale, looking north to Gouthwaite reservoir

After a brief flirtation with commercial expansion in the 18th and 19th centuries, lovely Nidderdale relinquished its lead mining and flax industries, using its considerable charms to attract an increasing number of tourists. Watered by the trout and grayling filled Nidd, this extensive, well-wooded dale is surrounded on all sides by commanding heights giving stupendous views of the surrounding countryside.

Habitat and birdlife rich, this walk is a must for ornithologists, the diversity of species likely to be encountered ranging from kingfisher and dipper to grouse and golden plover. In the past golden eagle have also been seen in the area.

The starting point for the walk is the Royal Oak inn in Dacre Banks. A tucked away sort of place with a lazy atmosphere and views of the distant water meadows, the traditionally furnished bed and breakfast inn serves Theakson and Tetley ales and home-cooked staples such as steak and kidney pie, ham and mushroom pie, roast rack of lamb and local trout. Opening times on Monday to Saturday are 12 noon to 3 pm and 5 pm to 11 pm. Sunday hours are 12 noon to 3 pm and 7 pm to 10.30 pm. Telephone: 01423 780200.

- **HOW TO GET THERE:** The easiest route to Dacre Banks is from Harrogate on the B6165 heading for Pateley Bridge. Turn left in Summer Bridge on the B6451, crossing over the Nidd and passing the timber yard on the right.
- **PARKING:** Park in the designated and signposted free car park opposite the Royal Oak, going left down Oak Lane.
- **LENGTH OF THE WALK:** 6 miles. Map: OS Landranger 99 Northallerton and Ripon (inn GR 197621).

THE WALK

1. Turn left from the car park down Oak Lane and go next right on the footway, passing Holy Trinity church on the left. Continue towards the wood yard (the site of a former water mill; hence the weir upstream) and go left just before the mill, following a public footpath sign to Glasshouses. Turn right at the mill perimeter towards the river and go left, crossing a feeder stream on a little bridge. Walk on past the weir and go left over a stile, crossing the narrow neck of a field and cross a wall using the through stones, going right on a track. Continue on the track, walking parallel with the old railway embankment, and go through the Forestry Commission gate and the Nidderdale Forestry compound, swinging left into the wood. Go through the gate and leave the wood, following the hedgeline, walking through another gate and continuing on a rough track wallside towards Harewell Hall on the right.

2. Opposite the hall, swing left on the access track over the cattle grid, passing a small pond on the left, to a junction. Swing right downhill on the lane towards Glasshouses, going right, in the bottom, over the river bridge into the village.

The fine stone building to the right is the 19th century former

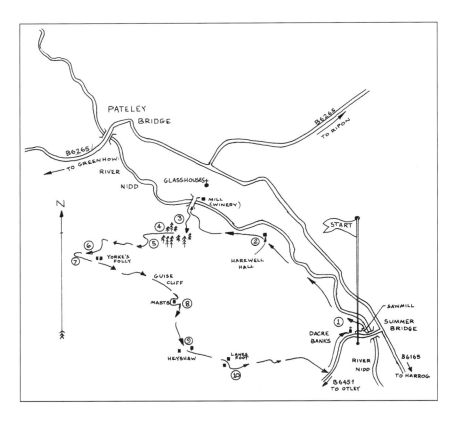

Glasshouses Flax Mill. Now imaginatively occupied by Yorkshire Country Wines, the mill is a winery, producing traditional English varieties like elderberry, elderflower and dandelion.

Retrace your steps, re-cross the bridge, go first left uphill and turn first right, again climbing, passing Low Fold.

3. Ascend and bear left, passing Hollin House Farm and going straight ahead, following the yellow arrow marker on the gatepost. Swing left past Bobbin Mill cottage and walk on between a fence and a dry stone wall up to the edge of a wood. Go up the steps.

4. Turn right, following the wall, snaking your way through the wood and going generally right. Go right at the fork and walk on through the gate, exiting the wood and following the wall down to a track.

5. Go left on the track, swinging in a half circle back up towards the wood, going right, left and right through a gate, past the cottages to the lane.

6. Turn left on the steep lane and at the summit, turn left, following the footpath sign to Guise Cliff.

7. Turn left to Yorke's Folly.

Built in 1809, this towering landmark is prominent for over 20 miles. The benefactor John Yorke of nearby Bewerley had been so impressed by castles and monuments in the Rhine valley, that when an opportunity presented itself to alleviate hunger in Nidderdale, he commissioned the local unemployed to raise his folly. There were originally three columns designed to look like the ruins of a chancel window. They were known as the Three Stoops – one of the pillars having blown down in a gale of 1893. Wages were paid partly in loaves and partly in cash.

Leave the folly and swing right to the ladder stile. Cross left and follow the crest path past Guise Cliff. Cross a ladder stile keeping to the moorland edge path and 200 yards before the communications antennae, fork right, following the yellow arrow marker, crossing the ladder stile and going right, left and left again around the perimeter fence to a track.

8. Turn right, following the Nidderdale Way sign, on a broad moorland track. Swing left and right and go right by Hill Top farm through a gateway, leaving the moor and walking on wallside to a cattle grid. Cross and swing left into the hamlet of Heysaw.

9. Go left and left of the entrance to Heyshaw Farm, following the Nidderdale Way sign, crossing over a wall via the throughs, over a farmyard and over a fence, following the yellow arrow marker across a meadow to find a middle ladder stile. Cross and keep forward to the right of the hedge, going through the gate at the edge of the wood and walking on through a further gate to Lanes Foot. Go through the gate, following the footpath sign, and swing right by Lanes Foot Cottage, continuing on the lane for 400 yards to the junction.

10. Go left, following the Nidderdale Way sign. Drop down to the cattle grid and go through the wall gap, steering diagonally right and

Yorke's Folly

following the Nidderdale Way sign towards the field corner. Go right over the wall throughs, following the fence down for 150 yards, then go left over a stile, veering right to the next field corner. Go through the gate gap, following the yellow arrow marker wallside, and swing right going through a gate. Go left to a farm. Go through the farmyard, swing left and hard right downhill on a track, continuing on School Lane to the junction with the B6451. Turn left on the footway into Dacre Banks. Go right down Oak Lane back to the start.

PLACES OF INTEREST NEARBY

Yorkshire Country Wines in Glasshouses has winery tours every Friday and Saturday at 11.45 am. The mill's former steam engine room is now a tea room. Mill opening hours are Wednesday to Sunday 11.30 am to 4.30 pm. Telephone: 01423 711947/711223. *Stump Cross Caverns* – go up the steep B6265 road west from Pateley Bridge and through the former lead mining settlement of Greenhow – show caves filled with stalactites and stalagmites. Telephone: 01756 752780.

WALK 10

HEBDEN: MINER ROADS BY THE HEBDEN BECK

With typical Yorkshire gruffness and grit, the leaden heritage of Hebden and Grassington Moors is writ large in an abundance of old workings and crumbling buildings, healing grasses and trees softening the rather aloof and brooding landscapes hereabouts. Following an old prospectors' track with sentinel rocks all the way, our walk accompanies a beck exploited to the full during the Klondyke days of the last century. But Hebden's stream, now clean and unmolested, is home to trout and dipper. The inward leg of the walk climbs the valley sides, giving good views of the extensive lead mining area at Yarnbury and beyond.

A packhorse bridge over the Hebden Beck

The walk begins in the centre of Hebden. A few hundred yards away, fronting the B6265, is the Clarendon Hotel, a village establishment with a reputation for steaks and real ale. Its locally brewed beers include

Tetley, Timothy Taylor Landlord and Black Sheep. Opening times Monday to Saturday are 12 noon to 3 pm and 6 pm to 11 pm. Sunday hours are 12 noon to 3 pm and 6 pm to 10.30 pm. Telephone: 01756 752446. More ambitious menus can be found in the many cafés, pubs and restaurants in nearby Grassington.

- **HOW TO GET THERE:** Hebden is on the B6265 near Grassington. Approach either from Pateley Bridge on the B6265 or from Burnsall (going through Grassington) on the B6160.
- **PARKING:** The proprietor of the Clarendon Hotel keenly discourages walkers from leaving their cars on the hotel's forecourt area. Park in the village on-street near the public conveniences.
- **LENGTH OF THE WALK:** 3 miles. Map: OS Landranger 98 Wensleydale and Upper Wharfedale or OS Outdoor Leisure 2 Yorkshire Dales Southern and Western areas (start of walk GR 026631).

THE WALK

1. From Hebden village, walk a few yards north, back to the B6265, and cross to the left of the bridge and the Hebden Beck. Follow the lane forward – sign 'Yarnbury 2 miles'. Climb the hill (Nanny Spout waterfall is to the right), continuing through the dell to Hole Bottom. Go right through the gate marked 'Bridleway Only to Yarnbury and swinging right, cross the old packhorse bridge over the beck. Go left, walking on to a gate. Go through and continue on the track, passing the reservoir. See a further waterfall to the right. Go through a second gate, proceeding to a point on the track opposite the blue Yorkshire Water sign, looking out for an unmarked path to the right between two stone gateposts.

2. Turn right and go between the gateposts, climbing up wallside away from the beck for about 250 yards.

3. Go right, through the gate at the top of the field, following the footpath sign. Continue in a southerly direction straight ahead, walking through three walled fields until you come to Mossy Moor Reservoir on the left. Go through a gate and follow the footpath sign and the yellow tipped marker posts wallside. Opposite the modernised farmhouse to the right, merge with the track and walk on forward for about ¼ mile to the intersection of tracks.

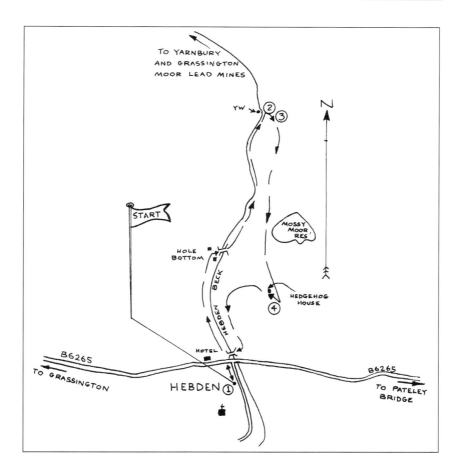

4. Swing sharp right on an arcing access road to Hedgehog House and just before the house, swing left off the concrete ramped road to the public footpath sign at the back of the house. Go left, following the sign, and swing right under the trees to find a gap in a wall. Go through and drop down diagonally right through dense bracken (the path may be obscured) to a wall. Go through the gap and veer right again, dropping down for a further 50 yards to a third wall gap and ladder stile, crossing and then swinging right and looking out for a fourth wall gap (in the direction of the village crossroads). Go through, leaving the bracken, and turn diagonally right down the narrow field, gradually merging with the wall. Go left, following the wall down above the terrace of cottages, and drop down off the ridge right to a signpost and

The valley of the Hebden Beck

a kissing gate. Go through and turn right to the bridge, crossing and swinging left on the outward track to the B6265. Cross and return to the parking area.

PLACES OF INTEREST NEARBY

The walk can be extended by following the track left to *Yarnbury*. Turn right here for another mile or so on the broad track to discover the extensive remains of the ore fields where flues, chimneys and some old buildings are preserved in-situ in a sort of industrial museum complete with interpretation boards. In Grassington is the *Upper Wharfedale Folk Museum*. Housed in two former lead miners' cottages, the museum tells the full heavy-metal story and contains many absorbing exhibits depicting local life. Open daily from April to October. Winter, weekends only. Telephone: 01756 752604.

BOLTON ABBEY ESTATE: STRIDING THE STRID

This walk from Bolton Abbey's riverside Pavilion Café and Restaurant is simplicity itself. Hugging the river it wanders upstream through the Strid Wood Nature Reserve to Barden Bridge, the return, with-the-flow path on the opposite bank following a similar course. The paths, through woodland thick with plants and bristling with wildlife of every description, are very well maintained throughout.

The Strid

Threaded by the often turbulent river Wharfe, whose notorious Strid has claimed many lives, the beautiful estate of the Duke of Devonshire is a model for conservation everywhere, its network of paths through the leafy river gorge, its carefully sited view points and seating areas, its arboreal management and colourful information boards having won a number of awards. Swirling with romance and legend, Bolton Abbey, whose centrepiece is the brooding ruined priory founded in 1151, continues to attract artists, poets and photographers and on busy summer days the river bays and tiny beaches get crowded. The Wharfe, a green, voluptuous and, in one respect, deadly Venus has a star rating that brings visitors by the score. But come before breakfast or in winter and you can enjoy one of Yorkshire's most exquisite landscapes with only the dipper and heron for company.

In recent years, the attractive and thoroughly modernised Pavilion – a fine venue for breakfast – replaced a wooden refreshment hut, an institution that for decades served only sandwiches and cakes. Today you can eat alfresco or banquet in style, the multi-choice menu offering everything from bacon butties to lobster. Typical blackboard listings include rosti potatoes with pan fried goat's cheese, rainbow trout in an almond, bacon and caper sauce, braised shoulder of lamb, and confit of duck with celeriac and salmon en-croute. The licensed Pavilion is open every day from 10 am to 5 pm; the restaurant hours are Tuesday to Sunday 12 noon to 5 pm. Telephone: 01756 710245. Adjacent to the Pavilion, in the gift shop, is an information centre giving details about the estate.

- **HOW TO GET THERE:** The Bolton Abbey Estate is west of Harrogate and can be accessed off the A59 at Bolton Bridge. Go north for about ¾ mile from the roundabout on the B6160, pass the Devonshire Arms and go under the ornamental gateway and turn right after the monument, following the car park signs down into the estate, passing the kiosk.
- **PARKING:** Park in the designated parking areas by the river. Fee payable at the kiosk. Car park closes at 9 pm.
- **LENGTH OF THE WALK:** 5 miles. Map: OS Landranger 104 Leeds, Bradford and Harrogate or OS Outdoor Leisure 2, Yorkshire Dales Southern and Western Areas (Pavilion Café and Restaurant GR 077553).

THE WALK
1. Pass the shop and information centre and enter Strid Wood.

This is the largest acidic oak wood in the National Park and the best place for lichens in the county.

Follow the green designated path down towards the river and pass the sulphur well on the left. Swing sharp right and pass Lud Stream Islands and the Stone Chair Seat on the left. Walk on and go right to the Strid.

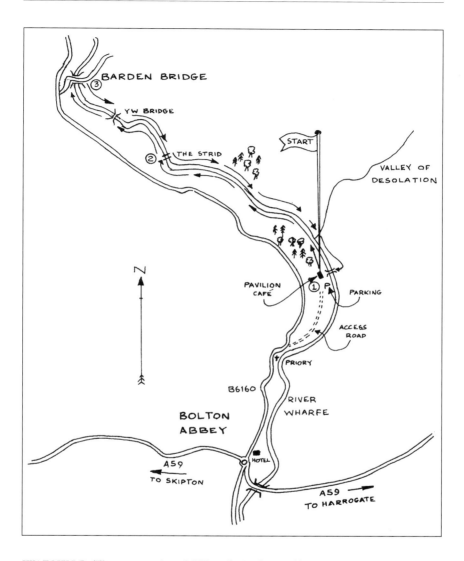

WARNING: The constricted Wharfe is funnelled at this point into a chasm just a few feet wide. The Strid, especially after heavy rain, is a magnetic and awesome spectacle, the 30 foot deep cauldron of water churning with foam and deadly undercurrents. Over centuries there have been many drownings in this dangerous place. Keep well back from the rocks.

2. Go back a few feet to the main path and climb up above the river and merge with another path. Barden Fell comes into view to the east. Fork right downhill and cross over a stream on a bridge, leaving Strid Wood via a stile. Continue along the water meadows path, going under the castellated bridge.

This elegant structure is in fact an aqueduct built in the 1870s by the Bradford Corporation Waterworks for conveying water from the Nidderdale dams at Angram and Scar House. Presumably, the sitting duke insisted on more than a pipe!

Walk on, crossing two stiles to Barden Bridge.

This genuine, three segmented arched gem was erected in 1659.

Cross to the opposite bank.

3. Go right over the stile onto the riverside footpath and cross a series of stiles back to the aqueduct. Climb up away from the river and cross a stile back into Strid Wood. Follow the well-defined footpath for about 1½ miles. Eventually it runs contiguous with the road. Keep to the footpath here, swinging right and left over a wooden footbridge.

The stream drains the Valley of Desolation.

Continue, following the direction sign to the Pavilion and Bolton Abbey. Cross a stile and drop down steps to the river bank and walk on to the bridge, going through a gate and turning right over the bridge back to the start.

PLACES OF INTEREST NEARBY
On foot, follow the Valley of Desolation (signposted) up via a spectacular waterfall and pool to the moorland eminence of *Simon's Seat*. Take a nostaglic trip on the nearby *Embsay and Bolton Abbey Steam Railway*. Telephone: 01756 794727; talking timetable: 01756 795189. Back, off the Harrogate road – turn left after Blubberhouses on the B6451 – is the *Darley Mill Centre* at Darley. Essentially a millshop, this free attraction based on the restoration of a 17th century water mill has one of the largest working water wheels in Yorkshire. Telephone: 01423 780857.

BILTON: THE GLISTENING BANK

Rising on Great Whernside, the Nidd flows through some of the most beautiful scenery in Yorkshire. Beguiled by its therapeutic springs, Harrogate never exploited the views and few visitors, even today, realise that there are far more enervating waters just on the edge of town. Our route accompanies the winding Nidd bank for over a mile and a half. Majestic trees and rare plants line the way. Dark pools, riffles, glides and cascades pour a heady cocktail fluttered by kingfishers, dippers and wild ducks. Children will particularly enjoy several sandy beaches that mark the Nidd's course.

The unspoilt village pub in Bilton

Bilton was a thriving village when Harrogate's only distinction was the smell of rotten eggs. The famous spa town has since absorbed its little neighbour but there is still a rurality and a distinctiveness that sets Bilton apart. It sits picturesquely, high above the Nidd Gorge, its undiscovered charms hidden by the thickest woodland and a commercial smokescreen that deflect the tourist hares to nearby

Knaresborough. Forget the bunkum that is Mother Shipton and her fatuous dropping well and come to see the real local attraction – the scintillating river Nidd.

Now raise your glass to the Gardeners Arms! Miraculously, it has survived a world that in succeeding decades gave us formica, chemical beer and frozen chips. Since I visited last – 25 years ago – the Gardeners Arms has passed into the hands of independent Yorkshire brewers Samuel Smith of Tadcaster. They have kept the stone flagged, low beamed, parlour type rooms intact and uncovered a long hidden inglenook fireplace which only adds to the considerable charm of this exceptional little pub. Outside, is a beer garden and play area.

The home-made menu consists of traditional fare such as roast beef and Yorkshire pudding, steak and stout pie, ham and eggs and fried haddock. Only Sam Smith brews are available – bitter, mild, a stout and a lager. Opening times on Monday to Saturday are 12 noon to 3 pm and 6 pm (7 pm Saturdays) to 11 pm. Sunday hours are 12 noon to 3 pm and 7 pm to 10.30 pm. Telephone: 01423 506051.

- **HOW TO GET THERE:** Bilton is north of Harrogate. Take the A59 Skipton Road through the town and turn right at the Dragon pub opposite Majestic Wine, proceeding for just over a mile to Bilton and the Gardeners Arms.
- **PARKING:** Park in the pub car park or on nearby Bilton Lane close to the line of the abandoned railway.
- **LENGTH OF THE WALK:** 4 miles. Map: OS Landranger 104 Leeds, Bradford and Harrogate (inn GR 315593).

THE WALK

1. Turn immediately right from the pub, following the bridleway and footpath sign down a lane. After about 200 yards, swing right through a gate on a footpath – Milners Lane. Continue on the well-defined track, gradually dropping down to the river. Pass the Woodlands Trust sign to the river bank.

Left is an old weir and on the opposite bank, the site of Scotton Mill. Higher upstream is the Nidd Viaduct opened in 1848 and closed for passenger trains in 1967. Near the viaduct is a flight of tiny steps cut into the rock face. The steps are said to have been used by the monks of Fountains Abbey.

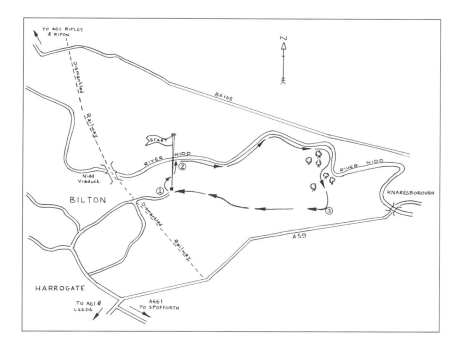

2. Turn right by the ford and continue along the distinctive bankside path using the track and duck boards and crossing a number of stiles. Pass the footbridge and walk on, gradually climbing right and away from the river, going through Oak Bank and Spring Wood. Turn right over a stile fieldside to Bilton Lane.

If you wish to visit Knaresborough turn left here.

3. Turn right along the lane (no traffic), passing the caravan site back to the pub.

PLACES OF INTEREST NEARBY

Harrogate has a multiplicity of attractions, not least the magnificent swarded *Stray* and its flower gardens. The *Royal Pump Room Museum*, housed in the original pump room of 1842, traces Harrogate's spa past. Try a glass of the poison that made the town famous. The museum is open from Monday to Saturday 10 am to 5 pm and Sunday 2 pm to 5 pm. Telephone: 01423 503340.

ILKLEY: '. . . AND DON'T FORGET YOUR HAT!'

Yorkshire folk have infiltrated every country in the world, their county anthem puzzling natives from Tipperary to Timbukto. And what an anthem! Sing to me a more jolly and melodious song about death and cannibalism and I'll eat my hat!

With panoramic views of Wharfedale and Ilkley Moor, our walk follows the river esplanade on the prosperous north bank, weaving upwards beckside along quiet tracks and woodland paths to High Austby. The return circuit passes Middleton Lodge - a centre for religious reflection and contemplation - and drops down through the delightful Coppy Wood to a watery finish. Bring your swimming attire for a summer dip in The Lido. After passing the pool, the path leads on to rejoin the river margins, returning over the bridge to the start.

Ilkley bridge

Ilkley is richly endowed, its towering moor, grassy riverside walks and fashionable shops evoking more the atmosphere of Baden-Baden than the West Riding. Like the German town, this 'Malvern of the North' had its spa, the health-giving waters attracting wealthy Victorians who built hydropathic establishments and prestigious hotels in the 1840s. The town expanded again between the wars when wealthy wool merchants commissioned baronial-style mansions that still grace the hillsides.

Refreshment options in Ilkley are legion, inns, restaurants, café bars, bistros and take-aways occupying every street and alley. But if you're after a treat as genuine as a chorus from that song, there is only one choice. Head for Betty's Tearooms on The Grove. A traditional emporium established in 1919, it is distinguished by serving ladies in old fashioned black skirts and lace blouses, serving soups and snacks and sensational fat rascals, Yorkshire curds, speciality cakes, tarts, flans and breads. Telephone: 01943 608029.

- **HOW TO GET THERE:** Ilkley is north-west of Leeds and Bradford on the A65.
- **PARKING:** In the large Pay and Display car park in the centre of the town off West Street.
- **LENGTH OF THE WALK:** 3 miles. Map: OS Landranger 104 Leeds, Bradford and Harrogate (car park GR 116475).

THE WALK

1. Go right from the car park down West Street and turn left on Brook Street to the junction with the A65. Cross the major road with care and continue going straight forward downhill past, on the left, the church of All Saints and the site of the Roman fort of Olicana.

Originally consisting of a clay rampart with stone foundations and timber gateways, the fort covered some two acres in extent. It was garrisoned by detachments of the Ninth Legion and by the Second Cohort of the Lingones. Interpretation boards show its layout and, in the Manor House and Art Gallery near the church, excavated artefacts may be seen.

Cross the Wharfe bridge, built in 1904.

2. Some 20 yards after the palisade, go left onto the riverside footpath

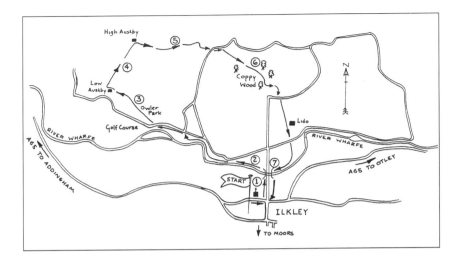

and continue along the bank to the next bridge, swinging sharp right along the bank and going left to the neck of the golf course.

3. At the sub station, swing right, cross Nessfield Road and go left uphill on the quiet lane signposted 'Owler Park Road'. The views left from here are almost alpine. At the top of the development by the Austby sign, go left, following the public footpath sign to Nessfield through a wood. At the edge of the wood, cross a stile and go left, following a yellow arrow marker over a sloping field. Cross a tumbled down stone bridge and veer right, following the Gill Beck in front of Low Austby House. Go left over a stile, swinging left uphill at the edge of the copse to a second stile. Cross, drop down to a bridge and cross, going left at the back of Low Austby.

4. In the field corner, turn hard right and walk uphill alongside a young plantation on a track signposted on a board to High Austby. Cross a stile and keep going uphill. Cross another stile and go through a gate, arcing to the right of High Austby. Swing left to find a gap in the wall alongside the access drive. Go through and follow the drive down for 50 yards.

5. Turn right on the quiet lane and follow the signposted public footpath straight forward to Middleton. Swing left and continue on the lane, swinging right at the end of the wood past the cottages and going left near Middleton Lodge retreat centre to the road junction. Turn left for 30 yards.

On the left, tilted and abandoned, is a precious and amusing tablet of communication history. The mason who fashioned the old milestone ran out of space and chiselled 'To Keigh –'.

6. Turn right on the lane signposted to Middleton and continue for 200 yards, going right over a stile and veering left in the general direction of the prominent Cow and Calf Rocks on the skyline to the left, to Coppy Wood. Cross the stile into the wood and swing right and left, swinging right at the junction down the steps. Follow the 'Woodland Walk' sign left along the boardwalk and the gravelled track to the next signboard to 'Ilkley', continuing on a right-hand path downhill on sleepered steps to a kissing gate. Go through and turn left on the lane for 50 yards and turn right opposite 'The Spinney' through a gap in the fence down steps over the beck, going straight forward past The Lido. Cross the road and go through a gap in the fence alongside the playing fields to the river bank.

7. Turn right along the bank to the bridge. Cross the bridge left and retrace your steps back to the parking area.

Places of Interest Nearby

The *Manor House Art Gallery and Museum* in Castle Yard is a 16th and 17th century building on the site of the Roman fort. It displays kitchen furniture, archaeological remains and local history items detailing Ilkley's fame as a spa town in the 19th century. Opening times are Wednesday to Saturday 11 am to 5 pm and Sunday 1 pm to 4 pm. Admission is free. Telephone: 01943 600066.

No visit to Ilkley would be complete without a trek up to the famous *moor*. Throw off your cap in wild abandon, fill your lungs with the heather scented air and join with me in the rendition.

'Where has tha bin since I saw thee?
On Ilkla Moor baht 'at. . .'

GOLDEN ACRE PARK AT BRAMHOPE: LAKESIDE STROLLING

On boardwalks, our winding path first traverses a bog land nature reserve – the best example of a 'wet valley alder wood in West Yorkshire'. Here you can see sparrow hawk, marsh tit, great spotted woodpecker and other colourful birds. The track leads on to an abandoned ornamental lake, returning through the marsh to Golden Acre Park with its pretty formal gardens, its large lake and raucous collection of waterfowl.

Golden Acre Park

In the halcyon period before the Second World War, these pleasant two acres were devoted to fun. For an admission fee of 2d, the last amusement park in the West Riding offered a dance hall, a boating lake complete with a pagoda, water chute and fountain, an open air swimming pool, aviaries, pitch and putt and a miniature railway. Today the park and the adjoining Breary Marsh are given over to plants and birds.

Since its closure in 1938 and its subsequent acquisition by the local authority in 1945, the Park has been successively landscaped and replanted and visitors can now enjoy its network of inter-twining footpaths, rustic bridges and woodland walks. Golden Acre has recently embarked on a series of horticultural ventures and is particularly noted for its demonstration garden where new plant varieties and growing techniques are pioneered. The green-fingered can also inspect the exotics in the Blenheim Courtyard glasshouse and the collection of ericas in the heather garden.

No amusement park was complete without a café and the modern Golden Acre keeps up the grand tradition in providing the homely Bakery near the rock garden, its cosy interior recalling the pre-war days in a gallery of nostalgic black and white photographs, old handbills and an interesting mural that covers the whole of one wall. The café serves excellent cakes, snacks and more substantial lunches such as leek and smoky bacon bake, filled Yorkshire puddings and jacket potatoes. Sunday lunches are popular. The Bakery is open every day from 10.30 am to 5 pm (earlier in winter). Telephone: 0113 2613064.

- **HOW TO GET THERE:** Golden Acre Park is on the outskirts of Bramhope, 6 miles north-west of Leeds city centre, on the A660.
- **PARKING:** Park opposite Golden Acre in the large official free car park.
- **LENGTH OF THE WALK:** 2 miles. Map: OS Landranger 104 Leeds, Bradford and Harrogate (start of walk GR 266418).

THE WALK

1. Head south and left over the car park to the corner near the pedestrian underpass and swing hard right over the boardwalk into Breary Marsh Nature Reserve.

The interpretation board on the left gives details of local plant and bird species in this Site of Special Scientific Interest.

Where the boardwalk ends, follow the wide path through the wood, veering left to the wall and fence. Follow the yellow arrow marker and the LCW (Leeds Country Way) owl sign and continue at the edge of the wood to the bridleway sign. Go right over the stream bridge and turn left to the corner of the lake.

2. Walk round the lake in a clockwise direction – the path wanders a

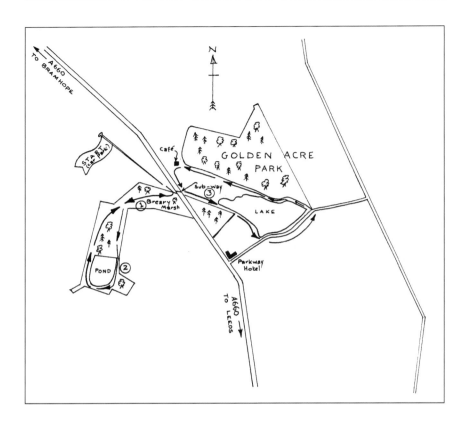

little from the edge – and veer left from the lake edge at the far side, picking up a track and re-entering the wood. Walk on, steering generally right.

On the left is a derelict farmhouse. It is interesting to muse on the fact that just a few short years ago this part of Leeds was in the depths of the country.

Continue to a bridge over a stream and cross, following the public bridleway sign back to the boardwalk. Return to the underpass.

3. Go straight forward under the underpass into Golden Acre Park and go right on a path, swinging left and continuing towards the lake. Veer right at the interpretation board.

A restful spot in the park

This will help you to identify the numerous and far from shy flocks of mallard, teal, shoveler, Egyptian and Canada geese, wood duck, great crested grebe and swan.

Swing right on the path and go left along the lake's edge, going left again over a stone bridge through the more formal gardens to the rock garden, the Bakery and, nearby, the Blenheim Courtyard hothouse and the demonstration garden. Go left back to the underpass and turn right, under the road and back to the car park.

PLACES OF INTEREST NEARBY

Adel Woods, just south of Golden Acre Park. Leafy walks and monolithic stones that inspired the sculptor Henry Moore. Also at Adel, *St John the Baptist church*. Nikolaus Pevsner never got overly excited in any of his architectural descriptions, but he says of Adel church: 'One of the best and most complete village churches in Yorkshire.' The famous door knocker is unmissable. To round off a cheap day out, take a leaf out of my book and treat the kids to a free display of aeronautics. There is an observation lounge at the nearby *Leeds and Bradford Airport*.

HAREWOOD AND WEETON: TALLY HO! ALONG THE WHARFE

Like a Fabergé jewel. Harewood has the finest of settings, its grand house, ruined castle and extensive parkland commanding exquisite views of Alms Cliff Crag, Arthington Viaduct and the Wharfe valley. In this Rolls Royce of a landscape, it is heartening to discover that the outward route from the village on estate roads is largely reserved for the boot. After dropping down to the river, our waterside track then follows the banks to an archaeological mound known as Rougemont – supposedly the site of a castle raised by the Lords de L'Isle – and on to the sleepy hamlet of Weeton. Completing a grand circular tour, the return path accompanies the river below the 18th century Harewood Bridge, before returning up the hill to the village. The whole of this walk is through Bramham Moor Hunt country and, like me, you may encounter the chase along the way.

Looking towards Wharfedale from Harewood

An elegant model village astride the busy Leeds to Harrogate road, Harewood is dominated by the magnificent house built in 1759 for Mr Edward Lascelles to designs by John Carr. In a heroic landscape fashioned by Capability Brown, the mansion has the richest collection of Chippendale furniture in the world together with superb Adam ceilings and plasterwork. It was erected on the site of Gawthorpe Hall, once the residence of the Lord Chief Justice of England, Sir William Gascoigne, who sent the future Henry V to prison for contempt of court. The famous judge was buried in the estate's ancient church where his monument may be seen.

The fashionable and recently refurbished Harewood Arms is on the main road, nearly opposite the current 7th Earl's monumental front gates. Stone built and furnished with soft chairs, polished wood and royal photographs echoing the intimacies of his lordship's private study, this conveniently placed and well patronised hotel offers both bar and restaurant meals. The extensive combination of food includes such dishes as queen scallops, baked smoked haddock, salmon and potato cakes, speciality chicken and bacon en croute, pork and bacon roll with provençale sauce, spicy lamb kebabs, vegetable risotto with crispy polenta, Mediterranean vegetable filo tart, lamb meatballs with herb dumplings and traditional grills and Sunday roasts. Breakfasts and 'elevenses' are available until noon each day and cream teas are offered in season. The house ales are from the privately owned Sam Smith brewery – Old Brewery and Sovereign bitters. Opening times are 11 am to 11 pm daily. Telephone: 0113 2886566.

- **HOW TO GET THERE:** Harewood is on the A61 between Leeds and Harrogate.
- **PARKING:** Park in the inn car park to the rear. This is operated by a barrier system whereby spending customers are given a token. On street parking, opposite Harewood House, is also possible. Otherwise, park on street in Weeton and start the walk at point 5.
- **LENGTH OF THE WALK:** 7½ miles. Map: OS Landranger 104 Leeds, Bradford and Harrogate (inn GR 322453).

THE WALK

1. Cross the road opposite the inn, turn right for a few yards and go left down Church Lane, following the public footpath sign. Continue going straight forward along the estate road at the 'No Through Road' sign.

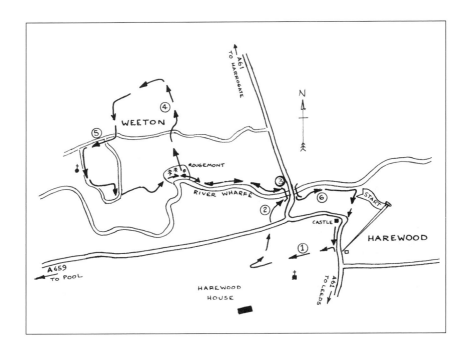

Gradually, the breathtaking view of Wharfedale unfolds. When you see sights like that, it's a privilege to have legs!

Descend between high grassy banks and swing right in the bottom, following the bridleway sign. Go through a gate to the A659.

2. Go right for 50 yards, cross the road and follow a public footpath sign straight forward over a stile into a field, walking alongside a stream and a fence, swinging right past the back of the farm buildings to a gate. Go left, following the yellow arrow marker along the side of a field to the corner of a walled garden. Go left to a stile and cross right to the sawmills access road, turning right to the A61. Cross (with caution – busy main route) and turn left along the footway and over Harewood Bridge and the river Wharfe.

The attractive four-arched span was erected in 1729.

3. Recross the road, and go immediately forward through a gate. Follow the footpath sign through a back yard and go left again through

Wharfedale with Alms Cliff Crag in the middle distance

a second gate to the river bank. Follow the bank right upstream to the weir.

The fragments of masonry and rusted gearing mark the site of an old corn mill.

Continue going right from the bank to a gap in the fence and go through, following the edge of the next field to a stile. Cross and go left downhill to the bank, swinging right riverside to a planked bridge over a stream. Cross, go left and swing right uphill away from the river, then go right at the side of the wood. Follow the yellow arrow marker left into the wood, go right and arc left.

This wood flourishes on the site of Rougemont.

At the next yellow sign, turn sharp right on a track and continue to the edge of the wood, walking on between two fields on a path to a lane.

4. Cross the lane, turn right and go left on the dead-end road uphill passing Healthwaite Hall. After 250 yards, go left, following a public footpath over a stile.

From this wonderful vantage point, you can see the whole route.

Follow the hedge down to a stile and cross, veering left over a meadow, steering just right of the big tree to find a bridge over the Weeton Beck. Cross and go left by the chicken run through a gate and go right over the parking area to a second gate, following the yellow arrow markers. Go through a third gate on a path between fenced fields to a stile. Cross to Brook Lane.

On the skyline to the right beckons a miniature Matterhorn – Alms Cliff Crag. If you want to stick your Union Jack in its summit, consult page 11 of my book 'Pub Walks in North Yorkshire'.

Go left to the junction.

5. Turn right on the footpath, walking through Weeton past the first junction with Gallogate Lane in the general direction of the spired church. Go left down the second junction with Gallogate Lane (it loops 180° left to the first junction). Pass the entrance to St Barnabas's church.

In the churchyard is the monument to the victims of the Dunkeswick Air Disaster – 24th May 1995.

Drop down on the lane and swing left to find a stile in the bottom.

At this point, I ran into the hunt. Had it not been for the intervention of an alert hunt follower who, as quick as a flash, snatched my Davy Crockett hat into the anonymity of his hunting jacket, this walk could well have been my last.

Go left over the stile and along the hedgeline to the next stile. Cross, following the hedgeline to the next stile and cross to the lane. Go right down the lane for 300 yards and go left, following the track signposted to Rougemont and Harewood. Keep going straight forward at the corner of the sewage works, steering slightly left to cross a humpbacked bridge over a stream. Veer left across a meadow to the top end of the Rougemont wood and cross a stile into the wood. Keep going forward, following the yellow arrow markers. Swing right by the fence at the far side of the wood and turn left to exit the wood on the outward route. Follow this back to the bridge.

6. Turn right over the bridge and go immediately left, following a public footpath sign through a gap in the wall. Walk on along the river bank to a gate.

The mysterious towers thrusting imploringly from the dense canopy of woodland on the hillside to the right, are the ruins of a 14th century castle.

Go through the gate and along the bottom edge of a copse.

Is the ruin to the right an aristocratic chimney?

Continue along the bottom of the next field and cross a stile. Turn right, following a track up along the side of the hedge. Continue climbing, going over a stile to the A61. Go carefully left along the verge to the 30 mph sign and cross the road to the footway, going left into the village and re-crossing the road to the inn.

PLACES OF INTEREST NEARBY
Harewood House is open from Easter weekend to October. Stately home attractions, bird garden, tropical rain forest exhibition, adventure playground, garden centre, gift shops, restaurants and picnic area. Telephone: 0113 2886225.

BINGLEY: AIRE MILES

The Aire is a John Wayne sort of river. It has a gunslinger's gait: it's time-worn, grizzled, uncompromising and, in places, a little dour like the one-eyed lawman Rooster Cogburn. But take the trouble to get to know the beast and it will quietly reveal its gentler side.

Beckfoot Bridge, Bingley

Over aeons the Aire has carved out a huge valley through the millstone grits that form the main mass of the Pennine Chain. Situated on the terminal moraine of a vanished glacier, Bingley was once known as the 'Throstle Nest of Old England'. It was pre-eminently a mill town, producing alpaca, worsted, dress goods and serge and, although the textile trade has largely disappeared, the legacy of old mills, chimneys, goits, canal locks, artisans' houses and cobbled track-ways remains – all built from a type of rugged stone that could best be described as Italian marble with five-day stubble.

Our walk begins just out of the town in the St Ives Estate. Originally known as Harden Grange, this vast, well-wooded acreage above the river was owned by the Knights Templars and the Knights Hospitallers who bequeathed the land to the monks of Rievaulx. In 1636 it came into the hands of Robert Ferrand whose family developed much of what we see today. During the Civil War, Roundhead officers and their general Thomas Fairfax were billeted here. The estate was acquired by the Bingley District Council in 1918. Our route follows a winding path past a pond and the romantic Lady Blantyre's Rock, to a place of legend above the Aire. As well as a site of ancient ritual and sacrifice, the Druids Altar was a noted Cromwellian encampment. The track follows the escarpment and plunges down to the river over a setted road worn down by generations of hooves and clogs. It then follows the sylvan river bank to Bingley Bridge, skirting the water meadows to Beckfoot where you will discover an old packhorse bridge over the Harden Beck. Somewhere near this delightful spot, John Nicholson, the Airedale poet died in 1843. He wrote:

'The winding Aire enamoured of the place,
Moves on so slow it seems to stop and gaze,
'Tis here the modest snowdrop first appears,
Drooping its head and wet with icy tears.
And here the primrose from its mossy bed
Silver'd with dew lifts up its lovely head.'

Refreshments en route may be had from two hostelries either side of Bingley Bridge – the Brown Cow and the Old White Horse. On our route the attractive Brown Cow is a champion alehouse serving Timothy Taylor prize-winning brews from Keighley and the lesser known ales from the Goose Eye stable. A locals' pub, it offers daily specials and is particularly noted for its 'sizzling platters'. Opening times Monday to Friday are 11.30 am to 3 pm and 5.30 pm to 11 pm. Saturday hours are 11 am to 11 pm. Sunday opening is from 12 noon to 3 pm and 7 pm to 10.30 pm. Telephone: 01274 569482. Going left over the bridge, you will find the Old White Horse, an unspoilt former coaching inn with original beams and open fireplaces. It specialises in home-made curries and traditional dishes such as filled Yorkshire puddings and steaks. The house ales are Bass and Worthington. Opening times on Monday to Thursday are 12 noon to 3 pm and 5.30 pm to 11 pm. Friday and Saturday openings are from 11 am to 11 pm. Sunday hours are 12 noon to 3 pm and 7.30 pm to 10.30 pm. Telephone: 01274 550961.

- **HOW TO GET THERE:** The St Ives Estate is about ½ mile south-west of Bingley (A650 from Bradford or Keighley) off the B6429. Look out for the signposted access road on the right.
- **PARKING:** Several car parking areas are available within the estate.
- **LENGTH OF THE WALK:** 5 miles. Map: OS Landranger 104 Leeds, Bradford and Harrogate (start of walk GR 094390).

THE WALK

1. From the parking area near the toilets, arc left on the road between the mansion and the golf clubhouse. Continue on a signposted bridleway past the old barns and swing right by the Coppice Pond on a woodland track, going left away from the water and right uphill to Lady Blantyre's Rock.

The daughter of a former mistress of St Ives, Dowager Lady Blantyre sat in the summer shade of this rock for over 50 years reading and enjoying the scenery. Her son-in-law has inscribed the rock to the 'sweetest of mothers'. Nearby, amongst the heather, is another monument, an obelisk commemorating William Ferrand, a philanthropist who supported the Ten Hours Factory Bill.

2. Veer left and continue alongside the boundary wall on a path threading through the golf course to a high wall. Climb over the steep ladder stile and turn right, dropping down on a summit track (or turn right and follow the wall down). Turn left (the alternative path comes left through an old gateway) and follow the sign to 'Druids Altar'.

The panorama of Airedale unfolds from this vantage point. Can you make out the famous Five Rise Locks on a near easterly bearing?

3. Swing left away from the precipice on a path, join a track and go left to a gate and cross a stile near a broken wall, continuing on a path through heather, dropping off the escarpment. Ignore the insubstantial paths to the right and just before the cultivated land and the gate, swing hard right on a rapidly descending snaking path. Cross a stile by a gate and keep going forward on a setted track with a beck to your right, going right and left to the bottom. Follow the bed of the beck and opposite Blakey Cottage on the left, turn right over a little stone beck footbridge.

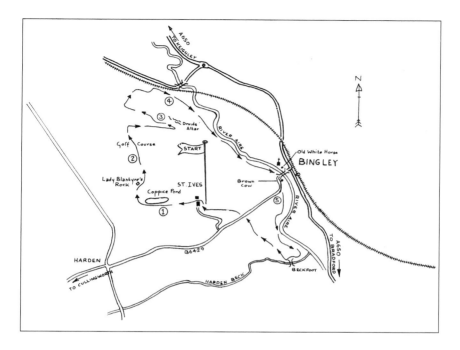

4. Cross a stile and proceed on a well-defined path, swinging right to a white gate. Go through and keep to the path under the wood. Go through a second gate, passing Cophurst on a track. You pass Raven Royd – a splendid restoration – as you continue towards Bingley and the weir. Swing right and left to Bingley Bridge and the refreshment stop.

5. Turn right with care along the B6429 past the Brown Cow for 100 yards and go left on a path crossing a meadow. Swing right uphill away from the river on a sleepered path, going left through the wood. Go through a gap in the wall and drop down left, then swing right, following a yellow arrow marker, alongside Harden Beck to the bridge.

Built in 1723, it cost £10. What a bargain!

If you can tear yourself away from this delightful spot, swing right to Beckfoot Lane and climb up past the converted mill buildings (there is another exquisite old bridge to your left) to the B6429. Cross and re-enter the St Ives Estate, weaving left and right back to the starting point.

The St Ives Estate

PLACES OF INTEREST NEARBY

The *Five Rise Locks* on the Leeds and Liverpool Canal in Bingley are one of the engineering marvels of the 18th century. Constructed in 1774, they enable boats to climb the best part of 100 feet! Also in Bingley is the *church of All Saints* with memorials to the Ferrand family and an unusual tombstone to Hezekiah Briggs. 'He was sexton at this church 43 years and interred upwards of 7,000 corpses.'

HEBDEN BRIDGE: ROMANCING THE STONES

Fashionable Hebden Bridge has the air of a gritty Harrogate but with oodles more water, two rivers and a canal figuring large in its history. Like the yellow brick road, the age-old packhorse routes around the town have surprises at every turn, the abundant sandstone paved tracks leading you to bluebell-filled dells, chasms, waterfalls and extensive broad-leafed woods. Our circular walk from the town centre follows the winding Hebden Water upstream to the National Trust's Hardcastle Crags, returning streamside to find a luscious refreshment stop on the towpath of the Rochdale Canal.

Gibson's Mill Bridge

On the packhorse route from Burnley to Halifax, Hebden Bridge grew into a thriving textile town in the 18th and early 19th centuries, the advent of the canal in 1789 bringing added prosperity. No visit to the town is complete without an inspection of the restored waterway, our walk fittingly ending with a short detour along the towpath to the Stubbing Wharf pub. Built in 1810 as a hotel, it continues to serve bargees in its attractive stone-flagged bar, offering substantial meals and a medley of real ales. This pub has a reputation for its large platters, typically filled with '1 lb of golden battered fish', a 'large helping of curry' and 'a large half roast chicken'. The daily specials board regularly includes dishes such as minted lamb pie, steak and ale pie and chicken breast in cider sauce. The pub has four mainstay ales – Flowers, Timothy Taylor Landlord, Boddingtons and Trophy – supplemented by a revolving list of four 'guests'. Opening times Monday to Saturday are 11.30 am to 11 pm and on Sunday 12 noon to 10.30 pm. Telephone: 01422 844107.

Another good walkers' pub can be found in the nearby hilltop village of Heptonstall. Serving hearty meals and Timothy Taylor beers, the Cross Keys is open from 11 am to 11 pm Monday to Saturday. Sunday hours are 12 noon to 10.30 pm. Telephone: 01422 843833.

- **HOW TO GET THERE:** Hebden Bridge is on the A646 west of Halifax. Best access is from junction 24 of the M62 going north-west on the A629 and then the A6026 through Sowerby Bridge and on to Mytholmroyd.
- **PARKING:** There are a number of free, well signposted car parks in Hebden Bridge on New Road, Hanging Royd Lane/Valley Road and behind Albert Street.
- **LENGTH OF THE WALK:** 6 miles. Map: OS Landranger 103 Blackburn and Burnley. (Starting point GR 985274; pub GR 982271 – adjacent to the A646 on King Street).

THE WALK

1. Walk along the main street – New Road – and nearly opposite the park, go north down Bridge Gate, turning left over the old packhorse bridge (erected in 1510). Turn right along Hanging Royd Lane and go right and left over a bridge spanning the Hebden Water. Pass the children's play area on Victoria Road and go right to the base of the old chimney, going left to the packhorse bridge over the river. Cross and go right along the bank.

2. Pass the old quarry to the left and at the bowling club, fork left away from the river, following the public footpath sign uphill and right. Continue past the old mill building to the right and about 50 yards

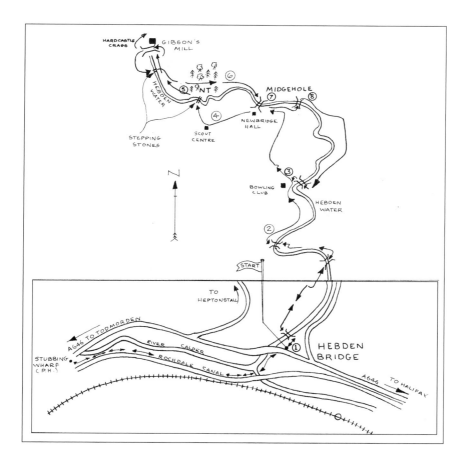

before the residential barn conversion, turn left up a flight of steps between dry stone walls for 100 yards. Turn right at the top onto a tarmacked road.

3. Walk on for about 300 yards and go right downhill into woodland following the 'Calderdale Way' sign back to the river and left to Midgehole. Pass Newbridge Hall and go left up a steep stony track, following the sign to Hardcastle Crags. Regain the tarmacked road and merge with it right.

4. Continue through woodland, weaving left and right to the Scout Centre, going up the steps and right on a track, following the signpost

81

The stepping stones leading to Hardcastle Crags

to the crags downhill to the stepping stones in the river. Cross and go left bankside into the National Trust estate.

5. Continue to Gibson's Mill.

This was built in 1800 as a water-powered mill. In 1833, the 21 hourly paid workers were mostly women and children, the youngest child receiving just 2/6d per week.

Turn left over the packhorse bridge and go immediately left onto the opposite bank. Recross the river on the stepping stones.

6. Go left away from the river uphill, following the red striped marker post. Swing right, again following the red striped marker post, and continue back to Midgehole. Cross the bridge right and go left along the bank.

7. Keep to the river bank, ignoring the outward track to the right and take the lower path, signposted to Hebden Bridge. Recross the river left using a cast iron footbridge and go through a gap in the wall and a wicket gate, turning left on a track signposted to Hebden Bridge. Continue on a track walking away from the river, passing a cottage to the left, and veer right to the lane.

8. Turn right on the quiet lane and continue for about 500 yards to Raw Holme Farm, forking right on a track below the lane. Turn right down steps towards the river and go left to the next bridge, turning right over the bridge to the bowling club. Go left, retracing the outward route to Hebden Bridge.

9. To visit the Stubbing Wharf pub, some 800 yards south-west of the town centre, join the towpath of the Rochdale Canal and turn right. Retrace your steps to return to your car.

PLACES OF INTEREST NEARBY

Canal cruises from *Hebden Bridge marina* off New Road. Telephone: 01422 845557. Just down Bridge Gate (near the start of our walk) the *Buttress*, the steep packhorse trail to the hilltop settlement of *Heptonstall* – interesting church and remarkably unspoilt cobbled village streets and alleys. Nearby, down the road to Sowerby Bridge, is *Walkley's Clog Mill* – traditional footwear sales and visitor centre. Telephone: 01422 842061.

HOLME: THE ROAD TO THE ISLE . . . OF SKYE

Even the breadth of England's biggest county cannot embrace the Hebridean archipelago but on this fascinating, high Pennines frontiers walk on the peat moors between Yorkshire and Lancashire we will take you to the site of the long demolished Isle of Skye Inn, its continuing legacy kept alive in the local name of the windswept highway that links the two counties. The walk begins in the hilltop village of Holme, the terrific landscapes hereabouts being familiar to all fans of the BBC series 'Last of the Summer Wine.' The route passes the twin reservoirs of Bilberry and Digley and follows the distinctive Marsden Clough to Wessenden Head Moor and the Pennine Way at the foot of the highest point in West Yorkshire – Black Hill at 1,910 feet.

The Pennine Way

The walk begins at the Fleece, an old drovers' inn in the hamlet of Holme above Holmfirth. Over the years its customers have generously supported the RNLI and the inn is dotted with lifeboat photographs and memorabilia. Popular with walkers and cyclists, the Fleece serves a menu that has girded the loins for centuries – braised steak, meat and potato pie, Cumberland sausage, mince, fresh fried haddock and a range of sticky puddings such as spotted dick. Ale-wise, the complement is Theakston's bitter, Old Peculier and mild. Opening times Monday to Friday are 11 am to 3 pm and 7 pm to 11 pm. Saturday hours are 11 am to 3 pm and 5 pm to 11 pm. On Sunday the inn is open from 11 am to 10.30 pm. Telephone: 01484 683449.

- **HOW TO GET THERE:** Holme is about 3 miles south-west of Holmfirth on the A6024. The best accesses for most visitors are from the M1, going south-west at junction 39 along the A636 and A635 to Holmfirth and from junction 37 going west on the A628 and north-west on the A629 and A635 to Holmfirth.
- **PARKING:** Park in the inn car park to the rear or on the street.
- **LENGTH OF THE WALK:** 5½ miles. Map: OS Landranger 110 Sheffield and Huddersfield or OS Outdoor Leisure 1 The Peak District – Dark Peak area (inn GR 108060).

THE WALK

1. Turn left from the inn back along the main road and go next left over the cobbled lane, passing the children's play area. After 150 yards go right through a gate, following a path signposted 'Kirklees Way'. Follow the distinctive path over meadows and through and over a succession of wall gaps and stiles, going forward at first and then generally left downhill, dropping down steps towards the dam between the two reservoirs. Swing right on the dam path between the reservoirs.

On the 5th February 1852, Bilberry Reservoir was breached, the resultant tidal wave killing 78 people and sweeping away 4 mills, 7 bridges and 27 cottages.

2. Go left at the end of the dam through the gate uphill and swing hard right uphill and then hard left, continuing on a track parallel with the clough (narrow valley). Swing right and go left past the old barn to the left and keep on the main path, swinging right and left. Pass Bartin (walkers' bunk-barn) and continue to Goodbent Lodge.

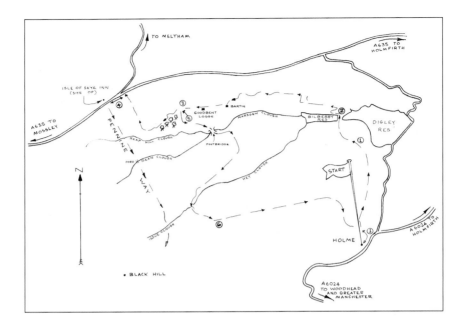

3. Continue for 400 yards past the lodge, mount the ladder stile over the wall, going left following the Kirklees Way sign. Go through a gate, skirting the wood of Reap Hill Clough. Cross the stream on a clapper bridge and veer left and right, walking up to the A635.

4. Go left to the site of the demolished inn using the broad verge.

The Isle of Skye was demolished in the 1960s. Its cellars can still be seen.

Retrace your steps to a point about 300 yards before Goodbent Lodge.

5. Turn right over the stile, following the footpath sign and dropping down left to a footbridge over Dean Clough. Cross and swing left uphill and broad right onto the moor, passing the grouse butts. Cross the fords and arc left to intersect Issues Road.

6. Continue on Issues Road track, going through two gates and swinging right into Holme. Pass the school and go right back to the inn.

A peat hag on the Pennine Way

PLACES OF INTEREST NEARBY

Nearby *Holmfirth* has capitalised on its 'Last of the Summer Wine' status and attracts thousands of visitors each year. See 'Compo's Café' and 'Nora Batty's Teashop' as well as other series locales. Brass band concerts are held in Holmfirth Park every summer and famous artist Ashley Jackson has his studio in the town. On the access route – A635 at Clayton West – is the *Kirklees Light Railway* with half-size steam train rides. Open every weekend and from Easter to mid-September every day. Telephone: 01484 865727.

BRADFIELD: AROUND DALE DIKE

Just a few surprising minutes from the noise and congestion of Sheffield, our relaxing walk starts in Low Bradfield, making a complete circuit of the Dale Dike reservoir through fields and woodland with soaring views all the way.

The Dale Dike reservoir

At 11.58 pm on the night of 11th March 1864, an earthen dam contained the 114 million cubic feet of water that was the Dale Dike reservoir. A minute later it didn't, the wall of water sweeping aside the village of Low Bradfield and surging down the valley towards Sheffield. The historic 'Sheffield Flood' killed 240 people and 693 animals, destroying 15 bridges, 100 other buildings and 4,000 homes. Repaired with more substantial materials, the sedate and almost alpine Dale Dike has been quenching city thirsts ever since.

Our walk passes the doors of the inviting Plough inn at Low Bradfield. A veritable museum packed with old tools, sparkling brasses and sporting trophies, this former farmhouse and barn has a baronial dining room for more formal occasions when the rotary spit comes into use, and twin parlours serving bar meals such as lasagne, steak and onion pie, halibut, oriental king prawns and various roasts at weekends. The house ales are Boddington and Trophy bitters. Opening times Monday to Saturday are 11.30 am to 4 pm and 6.30 pm to 11 pm. Sunday hours are 12 noon to 3 pm and 7 pm to 10.30 pm. Telephone: 01742 851280.

- **HOW TO GET THERE:** Travellers from Sheffield can reach Bradfield by using the A61 going north-west from the city centre, then taking the A6101 south-west for about a mile before forking right on the B6077 for about 4 miles, keeping straight forward at the Dungworth turn on the minor road into Low Bradfield. Travellers from the north should exit the M1 at junction 36, going generally south for about 6 miles to Grenoside, then going west on minor roads (extremely narrow in places) over the moor to High Bradfield and then Low Bradfield.
- **PARKING:** Park roadside in Low Bradfield on Woodfall Lane opposite the cricket pitch.
- **LENGTH OF THE WALK:** 5 miles. Map: OS Landranger 110 Sheffield and Huddersfield (start of walk GR 264918).

THE WALK

1. Go south on the road signposted to Loxley, then go left opposite the garage for about 150 yards and go right over a bridge, following a public footpath sign. Walk on uphill past the police house and turn right on the road to the Plough inn. Go left at the junction for 40 yards.

2. Turn right off the road, following the public footpath sign, crossing a stile by a gate. Keep on the straight path across the meadows and cross two further stiles to a quiet lane.

3. Turn left on this lane, winding and climbing for about a mile.

4. Fork right off the road, following a public footpath sign and yellow arrow marker into a wood and passing the information board.

You are now in one of Yorkshire's little known dales – Bradfield Dale.

Walk on through the wood and leave, continuing over pastures.

Boot's Folly and Dale Dike reservoir come into view. This tower was

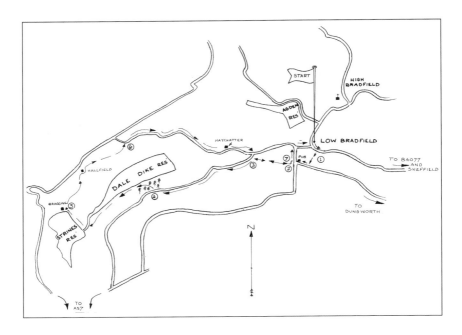

built in 1927 as a job creation scheme for out of work stonemasons who worked for the company of Mr Charles Boot. The current reservoir has a water capacity of 486 million gallons.

Take the right-hand fork downhill and veer right below a gate to the wall stile. Cross and walk on over two fields, following a broken wall down to a gap in a wall. Go through and drop down, crossing a stream bridge. Keep following the wall down, going right over a wall stile at the head of the reservoir. Weave left and cross a footbridge, continuing left uphill through the wood. Turn left over a stile to the right-hand side of the Strines embankment, crossing a stile to Bragging cottage.

The Strines reservoir, which was built in 1871, holds 513 million gallons of water.

5. Turn right by the cottage and continue on a path, going through an iron gate by the cattle grid, passing Stubbin Farm. Continue wallside, swinging left through a gate, walking on wallside through a gate, following a path down wallside to the Bradfield sign. Turn right using the permissive footpath around Hallfield, going left and right on its

The head of Dale Dike reservoir

accessway. Go through a gate and go left through a gate – 'No Footpath' sign ahead – continuing through two more gates to the quiet lane.

6. Turn right along the lane for about a mile, passing the Haychatter Inn. About 450 yards after the inn, turn sharp right on a lane, dropping downhill to cross a bridge over a stream. Turn left to rejoin the outward route, then go left over the stile into the meadow and retrace your steps back to the Plough.

7. Instead of turning right on the outward route, keep on here, going directly into Low Bradfield. Turn right over the bridge and go left back to the parking area.

PLACES OF INTEREST NEARBY
High Bradfield church up the steep hill north-east of the village is extremely interesting, having castellated walls, gargoyles and a medieval oak panelled screen in the sanctuary. Most intriguing though is the Watch House by the main entrance. This was built in 1745 to deter body snatchers.

WALK 20

SHEFFIELD: THE PEACEFUL RIVELIN VALLEY

Just a short bus ride from the city centre, this nature ramble passes the sites of the old factories, only modern signboards and a few tumbled stones, rusted valves and sluice doors marking the sites of the Rivelin Bridge, Holme Head, Little London, Upper Cut, Swallow and a dozen other water wheels. The paths are easy to follow and well maintained, the almost unbroken canopy of leaves, the succession of cool cascades and the constant sound of gurgling water making this special walk a delight on hot days.

The Rivelin Valley

Like orchids on rotting logs, beauty and the beasts of an industrialised past happily intertwine in this soul-land of Sheffield's history. Over hundreds of years, the Rivelin valley was raped of its trees and its waters were dammed, diverted and channelled to drive a succession of water wheels, their power producing corn, spades, scythes, cut throat

92

razors, steel strip and paper. But the slop of the great machines and the noise of grinding metal have long since given way to the sounds of bird song, the ruined goits and dam walls, the silted up ponds and the rampant reclamation of ash, oak, sycamore and waterside plants providing one of the most absorbing city walks in Britain.

En route, just a few yards from the trail, is the Holly Bush pub. It serves a medley of home-made bar meals, the menu including meat and potato pie, braised pork, speciality steaks, lasagne and fried fish. The house ales are Tetley and Marston's Pedigree. Opening times on Monday to Friday are 12 noon to 3 pm and 6 pm to 11 pm. Saturday hours are 11 am to 11 pm. On Sundays the pub is open from 12 noon to 3 pm and 7 pm to 10.30 pm. Telephone: 0114 2345457.

- **HOW TO GET THERE:** The Rivelin Valley Nature Reserve is west of Sheffield city centre on the A6101. Follow the A57, signposted to 'Glossop', for about 4 miles, leaving the built up area and going sharp right at Rivelin Mill Bridge onto the A6101 for a further 2 miles north-east to the parking area.
- **PARKING:** The Havelock Dam car park is just off the A6101, past the children's paddling pool on the left-hand side of the road as you re-enter the outskirts of Sheffield, two miles north-east of the junction with the A57.
- **LENGTH OF THE WALK:** 5 miles. Map: OS Landranger 110 Sheffield and Huddersfield (start of walk GR 324888).

THE WALK

1. Follow the dam path away from the car park, going left of the weir, crossing a bridge and swinging right. Continue on the path which gradually veers left to merge with the A6101. Turn right on the footway for about 100 yards and go right.

2. Cross the bridge over the river and go immediately left on the footpath, passing the first of our wheel location markers – RIVELIN BRIDGE WHEEL. Swing right past the weir to the Rivelin Nature Trail Board and follow the trail sign right past the children's play area, going left over a footbridge continuing along the river bank. Pass the HOLME HEAD WHEEL marker and at the LITTLE LONDON WHEEL marker, swing right crossing a bridge and continue on the path threading between the bifurcated river. Go left by the pond, climbing up to rejoin the A6101. Cross, going right for about 100 yards and go left.

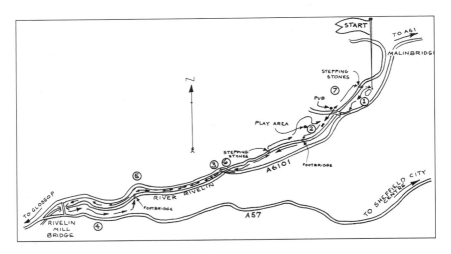

3. Drop down the steps back to the river and walk along the bank to the UPPER CUT WHEEL marker. Continue, swinging right over the bridge, keeping to the right of the dam. Follow the yellow arrow markers slightly uphill to the SWALLOW WHEEL marker, going right and left over bridges to the WOLF WHEEL and then on to the FRANK WHEEL markers. Keep following the nature trail direction sign ahead. Pass the COPPICE WHEEL marker and go right up the steps away from the weir and cascades, turning left above the river, going left at the fork back down to the bank. Continue on the footpath to the UPPER COPPICE WHEEL marker to the bridge which marks the outward extent of this walk.

4. Cross the bridge left and follow the riverside path back downstream, forking left, following a stone wall above the river. Keep to the top of the bank, arcing right away from the main stream towards the neck of a narrow valley. Drop down left to the brook and cross, steering right up the opposite hill to the direction post, following the yellow arrow marker forward. Turn left, following the yellow arrow marker on a gatepost, back towards the sound of the water, continuing on the path running parallel with the river. At the footbridge, go left back over the river to the outward route.

5. Turn right and at the next marker post swing right, walking in a left arc round the dam to rejoin the outward route. Continue on this outward route back to the A6101.

94

Water cascading down a dam on the valley walk

6. Cross and continue on the outward route until you get to the stepping stones on the left. Cross on these and go right by the weir on the opposite bank, turning left up the steps, crossing a bridge and going up more steps to the NEW DAM marker. Continue under the tunnel of arching branches and turn sharp right downhill back towards the river, going left by the children's play area.

7. Continue on the outward path to the bridge. Then, instead of following the outward path right, keep going straight ahead, crossing the road and passing the Holly Bush on a public bridleway. Recross the river on stepping stones and take the right-hand fork leading back to the car park.

PLACES OF INTEREST NEARBY
In Sheffield, is the *Kelham Island Museum* (illustrating the technology that made the city famous – everything from a 10 ton bomb to the 400 ton Don Engine). Telephone: 0114 272 2106.